G000038312

Published by Ockley Books Ltd

First published October, 2017

All text copyright of the author.

The moral right of all the author to be identified as the
author of this work has been asserted. All chapters written by
Richard Foster and edited by David Hartrick.

All rights reserved. No part of this book may be reproduced in
any form without prior permission in writing from the author and
publisher Ockley Books.

ISBN 978-1910906101

Front Cover, layout & design by Michael Kinlan

Printed & bound in England by:
Biddles Printing, King's Lynn

RICHARD FOSTER

OCKLEY BOOKS
.com

ACKNOWLEDGEMENTS

There are so many people to thank that writing an acknowledgements section is an exercise in glimpsing at the tip of the iceberg with the inevitable result that many are missing and I apologise to the vast majority who are below the surface. Perhaps the greatest debt I should acknowledge is to the game of football, which is so intrinsically beautiful but then again so utterly flawed that it provides enough material to keep hacks like me in clover and copy.

First and foremost I would like to give an honourable mention to all those contributors who have written about their very own Football Niggles so the roll of honour is Kevin Day, the only man who also contributed to the original The A-Z of Football Hates; Stuart Fuller, who has not one, not two but three pieces; Dominic Fifield, a fellow Guardian journalist and Eagle; Daniel Storey, the FSF Writer of the Year and author of the marvellous Portraits of an Icon; Ste Tudor, aka the Daisy Cutter and a fellow freelance football writer; Marc Webber, an ex-colleague of mine who is now a BBC journalist/ broadcaster. Also a big thanks to Matt Stanger, editor of The Set Pieces for allowing us to rifle through the drawers of their Pieces of Hate feature and pluck a couple of crackers from Seb Stafford-Bloor and Olly Ricketts.

Then there is Dave Hartrick, the man behind Ockley Books, who allows people like me to actually get our words published in an orderly fashion. His support, as always has been invaluable and he has also contributed his own thoughts on those pesky kids, those tricksy Freestylers. Next up on the rank we have ace designer Mick Kinlan and although I have worked with him before on the many editions of The Agony & the Ecstasy, I am still not quite sure how he does it but he manages to make my book rather attractive. Also Roger Domeneghetti who had the unenviable task of ironing out my grammatical gremlins.

Finally, the family who have yet again had to put up with me hunched over a laptop for many months, chuntering to myself while blithely ignoring their demands for attention, money or even affection. So Jessica, Amelia and Tristram, your father will be returning very soon and we can talk through your own football niggles which are respectively the ludicrous sums of money footballers earn, obsessive parents and whistling. And to my wife of 25 years Yvonne, you are a saint and I am very fortunate to have somebody alongside me who shows such fortitude and understanding especially when I am being weak and incomprehensible.

Until the next time.

By Daniel Storey

"Football is not ice skating," as Liverpool manager Jurgen Klopp observed. This is not a sport in which perfection is possible. Millions around the world may consider themselves as arbiters of their and many other teams, but there are no judges' marks. Only the result is king. Only the league table decides.

Barcelona, Netherlands, Milan, Brazil and Spain may consider themselves as coming closer than most to footballing Nirvana, but somebody will always come along and do things better or in a style that is considered groundbreaking. Little in football is truly revolutionary, merely a development of what has gone before.

Yet football is exceptional because not only is perfection impossible, it is not even desirable. One of the pillars of entertainment is unpredictability. By its very definition, perfection is predictable and so quickly becomes mundane.

For the neutral, there is more to be enjoyed in a team capable of astounding brilliance but just as likely to shoot themselves in the foot at any given time. Every partisan supporter wants their own team to win every match, but even they prefer victory against meaningful competition. Triumph through adversity leaves the sweetest taste.

This is true on an individual level too. The striker who scores every one-on-one by slotting the ball into the far corner is less popular than the one who rounds the goalkeeper with a shimmy and a feint. The central defender who strides out from the back and dribbles around the centre forward is lauded and applauded. We love the risk-takers and the boundary-pushers.

So important is the idea of flaws to our enjoyment of football, we reserve our deepest love not simply for the geniuses of the game, but those who toe the line between majesty and mayhem. These are the players we can affiliate with because we see them as one of use, humans as well as footballers. We see our own character flaws within them. These are not robots, but young people who have trained and practiced to hone their talent. Every now and then, the devil within them shows itself.

When we think of football, in those moments of daydream when lying on a sofa or sat on a train, we do not picture pitches of green carpet, pristine new shirts and identikit stadia. We think of mud splatters, sweat and great hordes of supporters moving as a throng in celebration. We think of refereeing decisions that made us scream blue murder and mistakes from players that made us question their familial heritage. We think of being freezing cold in

January, standing to get our football fix, and boiling hot in June as we follow our nation to the other side of the world.

This book is a celebration of those flaws. Some of the things that make you curse and some you may outright dislike. Yet they all form part of the fabric of a game that forever makes us come back for more.

Football is our escapism from the everyday, but we still need to recognise the travails of the everyday within it in order to become part of it. Like everything that we hold dearest in life, we love football because of, rather than in spite of, its flaws.

———

INTRODUCTION

A couple of years ago I wrote my first book The A-Z of Football Hates and whilst it did not sell as many copies as I would have hoped, it did ok and succeeded in fulfilling a lifetime ambition of becoming a football writer. The book prompted the usual mixture of approbation and antipathy but it served its purpose well enough and I was generally satisfied with the outcome.

One of the more critical comments centred on the title as according to those critics it immediately gave a negative image of what the book was about. People were surprised by the light humourous tone and felt that a different title would have encouraged a broader audience; the heart and soul of the book was a deep-seated fondness of football, which was exemplified by its range of imperfections. It was more about enjoyment and this needed to be reflected in the title.

Having taken this on board I am now embarking on a similar journey but under a new, less pejorative title. My publisher, Dave Hartrick and I struggled to find a suitable title for many months and in the end we plumped for Football's Flaws & Foibles. Flaws & foibles seemed more apposite because the words imply that they are still minor blots on an otherwise attractive landscape rather than huge stains on a canvas of negativity. Also such blots are easier to remove and one can imagine that some time in the future that such things will no longer exist, no doubt to be replaced by a raft of new ones.

There is no such thing as the perfect sport and if there was it would be boring as we would not be able to revel in those little annoying features, those very personal bugbears that cement our relationship with the game. So the vast majority of the Flaws & Foibles you are about to read about are more to do with love than hate. It is also in the nature of football fans to find fault in the game and hopefully many of the following will strike a chord within you whereas others may surprise you or may not have occurred to you before but now I have brought attention to them, they may become part of your footballing perspective.

As with The A-Z of Football Hates I have enlisted the help of a dozen or so aficionados of the game to contribute their own choices. I am extremely grateful to each and every one of them as they have given up their time to write their own pieces and each one provides a different angle to my own and is therefore valuable in adding to the kaleidoscope of the book's insights. I particularly enjoyed Dom Fifield's take on the tricky combination of being a fan whilst trying to retain the key element of professional journalism, namely independence.

Before getting into the main body of the text I did have to make an exception on the essence of the flaws and foibles as this entry is so much more than that. It is a subject that cannot be ignored and is worthy of its own place at the very start of the book as it stands out as one of the intractable problems facing football today. The concern is that a recent regime change has done nothing to dispel the fears that this organisation could eventually ruin football whilst its avowed aims is to promote and nurture the game worldwide. Ladies and gentlemen, I give you FIFA.

———

WELCOME TO FOOTBALL'S FLAWS & FOIBLES

Power tends to corrupt, and absolute power corrupts absolutely. Great men are almost always bad men.

Lord Acton

If ever there was one place where all the sins of football were collected in one place that would be in a secretive building on a wooded hill on the outskirts of Zurich. To be fair, I could have filled this entire book with the multifarious misdemeanours of FIFA. It is somewhat surprising that they have not used FIFA's headquarters as the setting for the base of a James Bond baddie as there are all the elements drawn together to make it as authentic as possible and plenty of suitable characters in place to populate it with sufficient quantities of evil. One can imagine all the meeting rooms having the appropriate names based on the seven cardinal sins – Avarice, Envy, Gluttony, Lust, Pride, Sloth and Wrath.

One has to hand it to FIFA, they really do outdo themselves with every move they make. They must have a right old laugh in the corridors of their Zurich HQ when they sit down to decide just how they are going to extend this incredible exercise in self-parody. Even following a change in regime when almost the entire executive committee was suspended, ousted or arrested there is still an innate ability to make extraordinarily bad and suspect decisions look like the most natural thing in the world.

So after Sepp Blatter had been well and truly Blattered when the endless suspicion surrounding his thirty odd years of having his snout firmly in the trough finally materialised as the Swiss prosecutors politely described it for "criminal mismanagement and alternatively misappropriation". Some of us foolishly thought that a change of guard would bring in some much-needed fresh air. How wrong we were. If we naively imagined that a post-Blatter era might herald something different then it did not take too long to be disabused of that fanciful notion.

The incoming president Gianni Infantino is no Blatter but then again he does not seem to have nailed the characteristics of a white knight either. The most worrying fact from Infantino's background was that he and Blatter were born in the neighbouring villages of Brig and Visp in the Valois region of Southern Switzerland. I am not sure if anyone has checked the local water supply recently but surely it is worth investigating as there must be something badly amiss with what is coming out of those taps.

One of Infantino's early moves was his proposal to expand the already-enlarged World Cup of 2026 from 40 to 48 teams, which did raise a few laughs until we realised he was being deadly serious. His justification was that "in a 48-team format, the quality would be higher because the 32 teams would have a play-off [alongside 16 seeded teams]. The quality would improve and not decrease in any way." Add to the mix that there is the probability that there will be penalty shoot-outs after drawn group matches to ensure that none of those pesky draws ever darken our door again and the future seems pretty much done and dusted. As Marina Hyde of The Guardian witheringly put it. "This is starting to feel slightly like the sort of World Cup my mother would design: one where everyone can join in and win a prize." And good old Gianni managed to earn himself a snazzy nickname in the process of dreaming up his childish scheme, ladies and gentlemen meet 'Infantile' Infantino.

Hyde assured us that her mother was an extremely kind person but the more cynical must have toyed with the idea that such an expansion could well have some sort of agenda that was not exactly open and transparent. It just may have had something to do with keeping certain confederations on board who might possibly be non-European. And those confederations might in turn reciprocate such goodwill come FIFA election time. In early January 2016 Infantino had his wish passed with flying colours as the proposal for the engorged World Cup was unanimously passed with not a murmur of dissension being uttered from within the ranks. As Infantino summed it up after the approval of the new format. "We have to shape the World Cup of the 21st century. Football isn't just about Europe & South America..it's global." I would humbly suggest that the perfect host for the 2026 Finals is staring us in the face and should not need to go to any vote. A country that ticks all the boxes as it will spread the gospel to an unexploited market in Asia and lends a certain freshness to the tournament. Step forward, North Korea.

FIFA is an organisation that could make a nest of vipers look an attractive option and the new breed are clearly not going to rock the good ship. Take the new FIFA vice-president and CONACAF president Victor Montagliani who had the sheer nerve to declare that "maybe the best thing that happened in football was Russia and Qatar." It may have escaped the attention of Mr. Montagliani that in the real world the condemnation of this decision has been as vociferous as it has been widespread. This is the problem that living in the Zurich bubble means you are clearly completely out of touch with reality. But that does not seemed to have caused too much concern previously and clearly does not have too much of an impact on the current incumbents who remain as away with the fairies as the last lot.

Montagliani could not have missed the fact that his predecessors at CONACAF did not have the greatest record of propriety. Since 1990 Jack Warner has been indicted for corruption, Lisle Austin was suspended and banned, Alfredo Hawit was also indicted and Jeffrey Webb pleaded guilty to racketeering and money laundering. Indeed in an interview with Reuters, Montagliani described the recent past as "toxic waste" so at least he is aware of the colourful history of an organisation the US attorney Loretta Lynch called "a criminal enterprise."

We have now reached the stage where nothing could shock us over the ethics of the bigwigs of world football. Indeed we must prepare ourselves for even worse excesses and abuse of power. The strong aroma of shit and corruption is not going away and may be getting stronger. Whoever writes the scripts for this lot needs to keep checking the relationship between fact and fiction because there is such a blurring of the distinction sometimes it is hard to tell which is which.

Of course FIFA did help us with this tricky dichotomy by actually commissioning a film about itself. United Passions was a disaster movie waiting to happen but not in the traditional sense of the word; it is no Poseidon Adventure or Towering Inferno. It is a film that even the director called a disaster as soon as it was released. "My name is all over this mess," Frederic Aubertin said, "and apparently I am a propaganda guy making films for corrupt people." The hiring of a strong, reputable cast including such luminaries as Gerard Depardieu, Sam Neill and Tim Roth did not save it from an absolute mauling. You know that things have got to a pretty state when members of the cast disown the project. Roth who had the unenviable task of portraying Blatter was not mincing his words. "The film is awful. I hated doing it."

The universal critical panning of this lamentable effort at self-promotion was not assuaged by huge commercial success either. On its first weekend in the United States the takings for the film limped to a barely credible $918, not enough to fill a brown envelope or buy one of those lovely Swiss timepieces of which everyone is so fond. One would have thought that if they could get one thing right, the great grandees of FIFA would have been able to make some serious cash out of the adventure. But this was out of their natural domain and boy did it show.

I can think of a much better premise for a film about FIFA, entitled "Shit, Lies and Corruption!" This is the latest James Bond film where our intrepid hero is up against the most sinister underworld organisation he has ever faced, run by the evil mastermind Dr. Blatter and his henchman 'Odd Job' Valke. Bond is captured early on and made to work in the sweltering heat of Qatar whilst forced to construct the Blatterdome in the middle of the desert. The further Bond digs the worse it becomes and in the end he runs out of options until he has to turn to the Americans for help to defeat the dark forces. Fact or fiction, the choice is yours.

Speaking of Qatar, there is another rich seam of controversy and condemnation that just keeps yielding more and more fuel to the fire, if you forgive the pun. The avowed aim of opening up new parts of the world to the pleasures of international football has really paid dividends in Qatar where they have taken to the principles of FIFA like a duck to water.

The latest development saw FIFA yet again facing legal action (they must be getting very good at this after all the practice they have been putting in), but this time the legal challenge is over the mistreatment of workers involved in the construction of stadiums and infrastructure in the Gulf state for the 2022 World Cup. In a slightly circuitous route FIFA have been asked by FNV, the Dutch trade union confederation to defend themselves against charges of alleged complicity in the mistreatment of migrant workers in Qatar on behalf of Bangladeshi migrant worker Nadim Sharaful Alam. Alam is seeking damages in the Swiss courts and if successful could open up the way for thousands of similar claims.

The summary of the writ states pretty categorically that "Swiss law, but also Qatari law and international law oblige FIFA to respect fundamental human rights and refrain from wrongdoing." The new executive committee, headed by Infantino might be forced on to the defensive as there has not been too much refraining from wrongdoing for quite a while now. They of course deny any such thing and claim they are not responsible for 'societal' issues and we can all thank the lord for that.

There is one redeeming factor in this farrago for football writers such as myself in that there is always an easy target for our poisoned pens. Aiming barbs at FIFA is akin to shooting fish in a barrel and is the default position if anybody is struggling for some hard-hitting copy. All you have to do is to check the latest shenanigans and there you have it - a nice, juicy 3,000+ word feature all ready to go anytime you wish. In fact they are a godsend with endless content available emanating out from the underground bunker buried in the hills of Zurichberg.

But perhaps the most risible of all FIFA's many excesses is the disbanding of their anti-racism task force as in their own words it "has completely fulfilled its mission." So just in case you were worried all is good and with their work done, it was time to move on, apparently. The searing irony that the next World Cup will take place in Russia, a country where incidents of racist behaviour are a depressingly regular feature of the landscape, has clearly not sunk in with the executive committee. In fact research carried out in September 2016 had shown an increase in the number of discriminatory incidents from 83 over the previous two seasons to 92 in 2014/15. By any stretch of the imagination that is a worrying increase but FIFA do not seem remotely perturbed by such a development, as according to their view everything is rosy in the garden.

Beneath this canopy of sinfulness there are the various confederations that also generally are up to no good with dark pasts and even darker secrets buried away. UEFA is probably the most powerful and has been known to abuse its power now and again. One of the most madcap ideas to have emanated out of their own Swiss hideaway in the anonymous surroundings of Nyon was the idea that the Europa League Final could move outside Europe. Run that past me again, the Europa League Final, which is contested by clubs in Europe, could move outside Europe. Well you have to credit the new UEFA president, Alexsander Ceferin with a fervent imagination even if his grasp of geography leaves a lot to be desired. "To go from Portugal to Azerbaijan for example is almost the same or the same as if you go to New York." Whilst the distance is not dissimilar, the very notion of playing on another continent is all wrong and especially in the US.

But Ceferin was not finished there. "China is financially interesting and the US is not just financially interesting, but football is growing there." Well bully for America. There is just a mild hint within this statement about the real reasons behind this move that begins with f but that is not football. Basically in the mad dash for cash good old

Ceferin and his mates will travel many a mile with barely a thought for the poor old fans who might want to see their team appear in a Cup Final. But as long as the game is growing in America then those fans can go hang as far as our brave new European leader is concerned. After all the NFL and the NBA come over to London for the odd game so this is just healthy reciprocation from the Europeans.

As long as we move the Final to a place where the game is growing then all should be fine, providing they also have the pre-requisite of lots of lovely lolly naturally. All this talk of transatlantic co-operation leads us seamlessly to the subject of the opening chapter. Welcome to Football's Flaws & Foibles and although it might be a bit bumpy along the way, I hope you enjoy the

ATLANTIC LEAGUE

Yes it's true. If we do not act now, we will see the biggest clubs grow larger and stronger while it will be increasingly difficult for clubs like us. Here it is still too early to talk about specific models, but the discussion of leagues across European borders is a theme that we look at and actively participate in.

Anders Horsholt, FC Copenhagen director

'The Atlantic League' - it sounds like a sequel to the Cod Wars, or a new division for the NFL comprising British gridiron teams alongside the AFC and NFC, or maybe even a new sports quiz show featuring comics from USA and UK. It is, in fact, the brainchild of some of the smaller European nations as a reaction to being frozen out of Champions League action.

The catalyst was the announcement that as from the 2018/19 season the big four countries - England, Italy, Germany and Spain - will be guaranteed four automatic slots each in the Group stages, and the less favoured nations were rightly disgruntled. It feels like the sort of response you would get in the playground when the tough kids started taking over and the smaller ones decide that enough is enough, they're going to play on their own.

Countries that do not have the necessary clout within UEFA are canvassing countries of a similar stature to form a breakaway from the top European competition. So the likes of Belgium, Denmark, Scotland, the Netherlands and Sweden are considering leaving their domestic leagues and going off on their own to form a brand new league and give Europe's leading club competition the coldest of shoulders.

The evidence is plain to see, over the last twenty years only one club from outside those big four have won the trophy when Porto beat Monaco in the 2004 Final. Remarkably that Final is the only one since 1996 to have featured any non-big four clubs. In 2016/17 not one team from these rebel countries qualified from the Group stages and the feeling of a closed shop has never been more prevalent. You can see why those other countries might be feeling a tad peeved. Indeed the Danish league boss Claus Thomsen was pretty adamant about the need to rip up the current Memorandum of Understanding that supports the Champions League and start afresh. "It is not an option – it is a necessity that somebody does something else," Thomsen said.

The concept has changed somewhat since it was first mooted and rather than a mini league it is now being seen as a cup competition, a direct alternative to the Champions League. There is a precedent as there was an attempt to set up something similar between the Scandinavian countries. 'The Royal League' ran for a few years from 2004 but unsurprisingly failed to attract any broadcaster and was allowed to wither on the vine. While I'm not sure how the marketing for this new competition is likely to go a strap line along the lines of "the competition for teams who were too shit to compete at the top level but deserve a bit better" may not be too far off the truth. Considering how disdainful most people are about the Europa League with the Thursday night jibe often hitting home hardest, this new venture would be treated in a similarly condescending and haughty manner, becoming the byword for inferior, low-grade football.

Nobody in their right mind would want to see more Europa League with the honourable exception of Sevilla who have made it their own personal property recently by winning it for three years on the trot. Effectively what you would be getting would be a weekly ration of Europa League-lite, which is enough to turn anyone's stomach and is not a particularly tasty prospect. There's not much appetite for simply more of this 'lower' quality football. The solution to a diminishing of quality has never been greater quantity, indeed the very opposite would be a much more sensible approach. More is quite often not better.

Breakaway leagues are nothing new, the Scots have been talking about doing so for longer than they have been striving for political independence. Celtic and Rangers grew increasingly bored with domestic domination and similarly envious of the growth of revenues and prestige south of the border. The original idea for the Atlantic League was mooted way back in 2000 when former PSV Eindhoven chairman Harry van Raaij dreamed up a similar scheme with David Murray, then owner of Rangers. I have an ounce of sympathy for their predicament but the solution is certainly not in the elegant bracket and falls into the 'if you can't beat them, join them' category.

The logical extension of such a move is that domestic leagues will be left with the runts of the litter and will not survive once the bigger and more attractive clubs have departed for pastures new. The very rationale behind those clubs breaking away will be echoing around the empty grounds of those left behind in leagues that nobody cares about or would want to watch. So the very motivation for the creation of this new league will have an impact on the clubs further down the food chain. There is a strong whiff of hypocrisy here that somehow these clubs have failed to detect.

One of the only redeeming features of this farrago is that it fits in so neatly with Michel Platini's idea that the European Championships of 2020 should be spread across multiple countries, where fans will become accustomed to the pain of travelling long distances for their games and racking up huge costs at the same time. So maybe this is all part of some grand project to reinvigorate the European aerospace industry whilst bumping up our rewards programmes with various airlines across the continent.

It would be interesting to see how the television negotiations might go for this. "Yes, that's right we are going to have all the second-rate leagues represented. All those clubs who can barely fill half their stadiums most of the time, playing each other. It's bound to be a cracking atmosphere and there will be millions gagging to watch on television."

Additionally the so-called Atlantic League is a bit of a misnomer as not many of these countries actually have anything to do with the Atlantic Ocean. Saying that, I suppose the North Sea League does not have quite the same ring to it. Why not go the whole hog and invite some East Coast American clubs into the mix? That would make it more geographically authentic at least and give a further boost to the Air Miles. Then what about the Pacific Cup? Or the Mediterranean Trophy? The Black Sea Championships anyone? The opportunities like the seas themselves are almost endless, surely everybody is going to lap this up on a tidal wave of emotion (or not as the case may be).

Then there are those national associations, generally the ones that are involved with such revolutionary ideas such as the Atlantic League, which have decided that tinkering with the simple, straightforward format of a domestic league is the way forward by rending it asunder. One of the first to go down the road of splitting the leagues halfway through the season was the Scottish FA and that 'experiment' has now been going on since the 2000/01 season. The curious element of this is that the first phase of matches involves clubs playing each other three times, meaning there is always an unsatisfactory imbalance between home and away matches.

Then the top six aka The Championship group and the bottom six or The Relegation group contest their own mini leagues but by only playing once against the other five. It again leads to an inequitable system as the home and away fixtures are skewed. The response of those directly involved in contesting this uneven, fragmented competition was not unduly impressed by the changes. In 2007 Craig Levein who was managing Dundee United at the time and just before he took over as Scotland boss, had been managing and playing in the Scottish Premier League since its inception described the format as "rubbish and a nonsense." Walter Smith Rangers manager at the time felt there was a conspiracy. "There's a hell of an imbalance when you see it," and he is right. There is something amiss when the team that finishes 7th or 8th can potentially have more points than those which finish 6th.

Other alternative competitions have been considered including one that has the backing of the president of La Liga to protect the interests of the lesser clubs. It seems rather hypocritical that this is coming from a league where the top two teams are allowed to negotiate their own television deal and the rest have to pick up the scraps from the table. Surely it would be better to look at the main broadcast deal rather than adding another competition, which is akin to fiddling while Rome (or possibly Valencia, Seville etc.) burns? With China's richest man Wang Jianlin also considering the idea of setting up a rival to the Champions League it would not be a surprise to see the whole of Europe fragment and break into tiny pieces. The sporting equivalent of Brexit if you so wish.

AWAY CALL BY KEEPERS

**Aloof, solitary, impassive, the crack goalie is followed
in the streets by entranced small boys. He vies with
the matador and the flying aces, an object of thrilled
adulation. He is the lone eagle, the man of
mystery, the last defender.**

Vladimir Nabokov

The position of goalkeeper is unique for many reasons. Despite
the latest development of the sweeper-keeper, which has blurred
the lines a tad, he still remains the only player allowed to use his
hands legitimately during the game and the one player who gets to
wear a different kit to the rest of his team-mates. The isolation of
the keeper from the rest of the side and the fact that any mistakes
are magnified (ask Robert Green, Scott Carson, Peter Shilton et al)
contributes to the general acceptance that there is indeed a tendency
towards madness. The classic line of "You don't have to be mad to
be a keeper, but it helps" is a truism that is very rarely challenged.

With long periods of inactivity, the mind must wander and even
though the very best show admirable ability to maintain high levels
of concentration irrespective of the lack of action, there has to be
some part of them that drifts off during the 90 minutes. During
these lengthy periods of reflection and introspection is when they
probably decide that the next time the action is in or around their
penalty area it is imperative that they make their mark. This is when
they dream up ideas about how to grab the attention of all those
watching and playing. They want to be the centre of attention not
on the periphery.

One of the key skills drilled into goalkeepers from an early age is
the need to communicate with their defenders. Generally the noisier
you are the better you are and nobody wants a quiet, mouse-like
keeper. In his pomp at Manchester United Peter Schmeichel was so
voluble that the back four must have developed not only a splitting
headache but also a fear of being singled out by the imposing Dane.
This sense of bravado has become as much a part of the keeper's
kit as a pair of gloves.

Inside the keeper's head there are voices and they are constantly telling him to be loud, not to hold back, and given the opportunity, to yell from the rooftops. Now do remember that the keeper has had a while to prepare himself for this moment and expectation levels are reasonably high that this will be offering some carefully considered insight. This preamble into the psyche of the keeper goes some way of explaining one of the stranger exhortations you will ever hear during a match and it is one that you will hear many times and every time you do it gets more and more nonsensical.

Here is how it unfolds and although it may have escaped your attention beforehand now I have highlighted it for you, please join me in railing at the sheer lunacy of it. I also would like to take this chance of apologising to you as this may now ruin some of your enjoyment of games for a while. It would be akin to somebody pointing out a continuous humming noise that you had not been aware of before but once you have been alerted to it you cannot concentrate on anything else. So again I am very sorry to do this to you but feel compelled to do so in the public interest.

The next time you are watching a game on television pay close attention to what happens at a corner. There will be the usual jockeying for position prior to the kick being taken with the added frisson of the ref warning players about the dangers of being caught holding one of the opposition. Beware anyone doing so under the beady eyes of Mike Dean. Anyway when all this posturing is over it's high time for the kick to be swung over and more often than not the ball is partially cleared and this is where we reach the key moment.

As the ball spins in the air on the edge of the box there is a defender underneath the ball and he is preparing to deal with it when the keeper comes out with the advice that he has been chewing over during the quiet passages of the game. There are probably only one of two options in the defender's mind but the shout from the man in green, purple or fluorescent orange gives that player the certainty and clarity of direction he has maybe been missing in his life up to this point. He does not have long so this message needs to be short and sweet, nothing elaborate or too complicated.

"Away!" screams the keeper. Away, as opposed to what else exactly? Away as in clear the bloody thing as far as possible out of my box. Now that is a good idea so rather than trapping the ball and starting to do lollipops inside the area. Such advice cannot be faulted for its simplicity and now that this small matter has been cleared up we can all move on. But honestly, how does bawling "Away!" actually help matters? Of course he is going to try to clear the ball, what else is he going to do with it?

In these days of possession football and increasingly sophisticated tactics there is only one course of action. Even John Stones, that doyen of the sometimes over-elaborate defensive play, would not be tempted to do anything but get the ball out of there as quickly as possible so he doesn't need Ederson Moraes or Claudio Bravo screaming "Away!", "Longe" or "Lejos". In a similar vein I am pretty sure that neither Moraes nor Bravo would appreciate it if just before they about to take a goal-kick that Stones turned round to them and bawled "Away!" They would probably end up shanking it straight to the centre forward on the edge of the penalty area who would calmly deposit it into the unguarded net. So much for the revolution of the keeper sweeper.

Or how about during a penalty shoot-out as each kicker is running up shouting "shoot!" and see how you get on. You will either get a proper shellacking, be sent off, or be chased off the pitch by an angry mob. Quite possibly all three. So let's drop this category of stating the bleeding obvious once and for all and banish this away call as an unnecessary irrelevance. Away? My arse.

It's very weird. All of a sudden it changes trajectory on you. It's like it doesn't want to be kicked. It's incredible, it's like someone is guiding it. You are going to kick it and it moves out of the way. I think it's supernatural, it's very bad.

Brazilian forward Luis Fabiano, clearly unimpressed with the Jabulani ball during the 2010 World Cup

It's an essential piece of equipment is the football. Without it the game would be properly stuffed so it might seem a curiosity to have an entry for balls in this book. This is less about the ball itself and more to do with the hoopla and hype surrounding the launch, or what has become the unveiling, of the obligatory newly-designed ball. I am not advocating a return to the heavy, laced-up medicine balls that masqueraded as footballs in the 1950s, but there is a feeling that evolution has got ahead of itself and leapt a couple of stages in the race to be ahead of the curve.

There was a time when the only excitement generated over how a ball looked was at the World Cup when every four years there would be the launch of a tailor-made one to get us into the mood for the forthcoming tournament. The choice of an orange ball for the 1966 World Cup Final is an issue that still concerns me, as I am pretty sure there has been very little snowfall in London in late July. The next World Cup in 1970 produced the most memorable ball. The mesmerising Adidas Telstar with its black hexagons shimmering against the white background in the Mexican heat accentuated the brilliance of the Brazilians Pele, Jarzinho, Carlos Alberto and their team mates. Those apart I have never been overly concerned about the ball other than that it should be round and generally kickable.

It has become as much part of the World Cup ritual as the unfinished stadia or the latest FIFA scandal. There is an imperative that a new style ball has to be launched and that ball must cause controversy in that its flight is as difficult to predict as the quarter-finalists. Remember the Jabulani from 2010, which gave all goalkeepers the cold sweats as it seemed to have a mind of its own as it dipped and dived just before reaching the poor old keeper? Ask Rob Green who somehow managed to allow Clint Dempsey's daisy-cutter to deceive him and squirm apologetically through his legs and over the line. Jabulani gone, it was time for the Brazuca in 2014 which had more technology invested in it than your average space rocket.

Back on the domestic front the very first splashes of colour appeared at the advent of the Premier League with Mitre's Pro Max featuring a series of pretty understated arrows (or maybe chevrons) which were then developed for the Ultimax, used between 1995 and 2000. Things have moved on apace and now for every domestic season we have the thrilling prospect of waiting expectantly to see what the ball manufacturers have been up to in their secret bunkers during the dark winter months.

Each year they look to outdo their previous incarnations with features that will have people fit to bursting to spend over £100 on this year's model. Take the 2016/17 Nike Ordem 4 as a prime example of this sort of one-upmanship. You may have missed the fact that we are now up to the fourth in this series. The fact that there does not appear to be an Ordem 1 does not seem to bother anyone unduly. Nevertheless Nike have been the official ball supplier to the Premier

League since 2000 so they know a trick, or maybe that should be a tick/swoosh, or two about how to whip everybody into a frenzy of excitement over a spherical object.

The ball is such an integral part of the whole match day performance that it even warrants having its own plinth from which it is plucked with great aplomb by the referee as the players and officials come on to the pitch. The ball is displayed as if it were a trophy itself in front of an adoring crowd. It is almost a shame that the ball has to go through the indignity of being kicked around the park as so much hard work has gone into making it look and feel so great.

Just sit back and wonder at the sheer audacity of the description in the press release for the Ordem 4, which miraculously blends blue, green and purple for a multi-coloured effort to ensure maximum visibility. Now there's a novel concept - a football that you can see. Let's take a moment to laugh at those old fools who just used to churn out plain white balls. One wonders what those ingenious technicians will come up with next, but you do not have to wait too long to find out.

'Developed for elite footballers, the Ordem 4 has been refined around three areas: construction, material and graphics.' Well thank god for that because just imagine if the three areas of refinement were much less wholesome such as anarchy, hot air and tiny specks of grit. Where would we end up? With a ball that unsettles the players and rattles their cages to an unbearable degree whilst completely disorienting the watching public. And it is just as well this is targeted at elite footballers, as am not sure what mere mortals such as those hardy souls who play the game for pure enjoyment such as the thousands of Sunday League practitioners would make of it.

This is just the (visible) tip of the iceberg as we go further into the nitty-gritty of the cunning genius of these most sophisticated designers. 'A new wrapped bladder system ensures the smoothest and most consistent surface – delivering optimal touch and accurate flight.' So when your team's agricultural centre half launches one of his aimless hoofs in the direction of the halfway line you may start questioning the very idea of optimal touch and accurate flight as the ball sails harmlessly into touch. Jesus Damo, have you not been paying attention? We have reached a point where there can be no excuses for a misplaced pass or a wild shot over the bar. This is pretty close to football nirvana.

But wait there is yet more to take in, such as 'the geometric 12 panel fuse-welded construction (that) employs a new 3D printed ink technique.' All those custom-made boots with pictures of the player's mansion /crib or their latest supercar inlaid on to the sole are going to absolutely love that panelling. As for the 3D printed ink technique bring it on, as long as it does not rub off on the magenta-streaked insteps, as that could get really messy.

'Finally, the ball's graphics follow the design principle of "Flow Motion", applying a luminance that ensures excellent visibility while the ball is in play.' Apparently the Flow Motion concept was born out of Nike's radical Radiant Reveal Pack, so beloved of all football fans everywhere. The bright spark who came up with the Flow Motion (sic) idea may need to be re-educated in a secure institution and never be released into public again, mainly for his own good, but that's for another time.

Also the last time I looked in the Oxford English Dictionary luminance was defined as the intensity of light emitted from a surface per unit area in a given direction. Call me a pedant but is it not a bit unfair to design a ball that is designed solely for one goalkeeper. I know Shay is getting on a bit and may need all the help he can get in his dotage but this is not a level playing field. One wonders whether he will be issued with special 3D glasses, like the ones you get at the cinema, to ensure he gets the full benefits of that luminance.

The huge advantages of this revolutionary ball are not just being limited to the auspices of the Premier League but they will also be busy ripping up the rulebook in Spain and Italy with a few ever so subtle adjustments for La Liga (a charming combination of navy, orange & yellow) and Serie A (an equally alluring mix of orange, pink and purple) versions, all with the appropriate league branding naturally. Then of course just as your eyes have become accustomed to this new luminance out comes the high-vis winter model, which ensures that as the nights draw in and the floodlights burn in the dark sky the ball can still be spotted by all concerned.

Sure enough as soon as we are in early October all our attention is drawn to the 'official release' of the winter ball, which for the 2016/17 season looked remarkably like an over-sized satsuma, ready to explode on to the scene. Maybe this is a throwback to the strangely coloured ball in 1966 and yet another chance to revel in 50th anniversary of that moment. But no, this is all about seeing is believing and it is an immense relief to us all that all those finely tuned athletes will be able to spot the garish combination of orange, yellow and pink from afar in the gloomy, brooding winter skies. The justification behind this blatant money making exercise is as visible as the ball they are pushing down our throats or eyes. And on it goes as the ball, the Nike swoosh and the whole show just keep on rolling ever so merrily along their way. I am sure that like me you simply cannot wait for what the Ordem 5 has in store, maybe they will come up with a radical new shape to really shake us to the core and take balls to a new, unheard of dimension.

As we are on the subject of balls here is a small footnote on an over-used and nonsensical phrase:

Raheem Sterling did very well for England and went past the opposition impressively, but his final pass wasn't up to standard.

Paul Scholes on Raheem Sterling's performance
against Italy in 2014 World Cup

There is a common complaint amongst analysts and pundits that it is the 'final ball' that lets teams down. No shit, Sherlock. This is not that useful an observation as by definition the final ball will be the last and if it does not end up with a goal then it can be assumed that the final ball has, to a certain extent, failed. When a move breaks down the final ball is seen as the culprit with possession being squandered but it is a bit like saying a man's final breath was not a good one. This is a self-fulfilling prophecy and like so many of its type it is of very little use to man or beast, ultimately. No doubt there are scores of data crunchers ready to digest and interpret this crucial piece of information but it does fall into the "stating the bleedin' obvious" category.

With so much time and money now invested in the analysis of football you would have though that the Final Ball had played its Final Ball but it is still being trotted out, left, right and centre. Amongst all the heat maps and endless statistics it is a bit of an anachronism to have this concept still circulating. If you do not believe me I can guarantee the next time you listen to a commentary, whether it is on radio or television, the expression 'the final ball is so poor' or a derivative will be used at least three or four times during any given match. This particular juggernaut of nonsense is simply unstoppable.

Maybe we can encourage the commentators and pundits to look forensically at the penultimate ball instead; that crucial one just before the Final Ball and quite possibly the very reason why the move ended with the next ball. Maybe the weight of the penultimate ball is not quite right or there is a fatal inaccuracy that killed the Final Ball. I long for the day when Martin Tyler starts saying that the penultimate ball was so poor. That would be a cause for celebration and rejoicing across the nation.

There is one shining example of when the truism of the final ball did not materialise. Taking a look at that famous Leeds passing move against Southampton from 1972 when Revie's team were already coasting at 7-0 with a few minutes to go and, as Barry Davies sagely observed, as this multi-pass extravaganza unfolded "to say that Leeds are toying with Southampton is an understatement." The move, which reached a pinnacle when Billy Bremner started to try the odd backheel, was only ended by the final whistle, a blessed relief to the Southampton players who had been suffering a death by a thousand cuts waiting for that dreaded Final Ball...

BRANDS

The fact that Prince William, David Cameron and Tom Hanks are fans added to the x-factor of the club. We have the ambition to take Aston Villa global and take it to one of the biggest markets in the world – China – where we are already the 14th most recognised club.

Keith Wyness, Aston Villa chief executive

Just like in fashion circles where red and green should never be seen so similarly the words 'brand' and 'football' should never coincide. Football clubs began life as the focal points of their local community and whilst this could not realistically remain their raison d'etre into the 21st century, the loss of that connection with their origins is one that will never be regained. William McGregor, the founder of the

Football League, will be stroking his beard and shaking his head in horror at what has become of those twelve clubs he brought together in 1888 and, in particular, his beloved Aston Villa if Mr. Wyness' remarks are anything to go by. He certainly would not recognise many of the facets of the modern club and the one singular aspect that would beguile him most is the evolution of the football club as a brand.

I am not advocating a return to Victorian times but when clubs become obsessed with their image, marketing potential, or international credibility it is time to call in the administrators because that club has lost its meaning and death is the only answer. Once a club becomes a commodity with the heart and soul ripped out and cast asunder we can draw the curtains. Chelsea's switch of kit manufacturers is a prime example where all the attention was focused on the size of the deal they managed to eke out of Nike to replace Adidas, rather than any consideration of the quality of said kit.

The headlines screamed about the colossal £900 million the club would earn over the next 15 years. Chelsea director Marina Granovskaia's official statement was telling. "We believe Nike will be able to support our growth into new markets as well as helping us maintain our place among the world's elite football clubs." The sole focus to develop the brand, which just as easily could be a soap powder or a fizzy drink. Ms. Granovskaia must be salivating at the prospect of all those customers queuing around the block in Kuala Lumpur or Hong Kong to spend a small fortune on a replica shirt.

You can always tell that things are getting out of hand when the marketing department starts to rival the playing squad in terms of number of people. Mysterious and exotically named job titles start appearing in the list of staff. Watch out for the time when the SEO Manager and the Marketing Communications Director first appears in the matchday programme as you will then be able to work out when the rot really has set in.

When clubs justify their ridiculous pre-season tour that sees them visit more Asian countries than a student on their gap year with the idea of reaching out to lucrative markets, the alarm bells should be ringing. This is the tipping point. The club medical staff may be pointing out the dangers of deep vein thrombosis and the myriad of detrimental effects on the health and fitness of the players from too much flying to anyone who will listen. They are drowned out by a gaggle of marketing suits cooing over the RPIs from the Oceanic region and the great impact on the core brand recognition values.

Life is so much simpler in the cosseted world of brand development where there are techniques and tactics that face no direct opposition and spreadsheets can rule the world. Indeed it must be frustrating for these guys whose hard work is now and again railroaded by those pesky players and their inability to match results on the pitch. How frustrating it must be for those guys beavering away on their multi-level strategies to identify those crucial USPs, to have them undermined by an errant penalty or a mis-placed pass.

Almost inevitably Manchester United have the longest list of sponsors and partners, stretching to the announcement in October 2016 that they had secured a five-year global partnership with the club's first ever Official Mattress and Pillow Partner, or OMPP for short. Apparently Milly were going to support "in helping with the sleep and recovery of players," by supplying mattresses to be used at the training ground's existing sleeping pods. Considering that this earth-shattering announcement came on the back of a goalless draw at home to Burnley served to emphasise the distance from reality and lack of understanding of how irony generally works.

If there was a club where the idea of brand development has overtaken and, to a certain extent, smothered the spirit of the football club, then Liverpool may well be it. With the usual raft of sponsors lining up to be associated with such a powerful global brand there are some pretty surreal link-ups with the likes of Dunkin' Donuts and Subway clearly making the most of their healthy images. When Liverpool signed a deal in September 2014 with the aforementioned Dunkin' Donuts to become the official coffee, tea and bakery provider there was no turning back.

Some two years on there was the point at which the whole sponsorship model started to eat itself when the club's official Timing Partner Holler sent tweets mocking the club for its lack of titles after Marcus Rashford scored a hat-trick for England Under-21s – "When Arsenal last won the league Marcus Rashford was 6-years old. When Liverpool last won it his dad (sic) was 10." Ouch. Talk about getting the wrong end of the stick, I'm not sure undermining the heritage of a club and highlighting the drought of winning a title is really the best way to build brand affinity.

By making football subservient to a vast swathe of marketing initiatives is asking for trouble as the essence of the club is lost amidst the cacophony of brand messages.

Karren Brady let the cat out of the bag when she suggested that West Ham's ill-starred move to London Stadium was "a real opportunity to change brand values." After all as the Hammers' vice chair astutely pointed out the club lacked culture. "At football clubs we don't make anything, we don't manufacture anything: we don't really produce anything other than getting more players," Brady explained. "So getting the culture right, being a place where something is expected of you, having discipline, planning and process and strategy. That wasn't there."

There is one thing missing from Brady's bold brand statement. There is no sense that she is talking about football. This sort of generic corporate message is one that you will hear trotted out up and down the country every day in the boardrooms of a range of companies involved in all manner of businesses. Football clubs do not adhere to the general principles of business. For starters only a very few actually operate at a profit and most of them would have folded or been sold if they were merely companies.

So for the sake of a cultural change there goes a hundred odd years worth of history at Upton Park, literally blown to smithereens as the ground was demolished in front of the cameras for a film shoot. What Brady does not seem to realise is that running a football club is not the same as auditioning for the next series of The Apprentice. When she was challenged about the success of the move her response was telling "we are ranked 15th in terms of brand values. We were 115th when I joined the club." So bugger the trophies or the league position as long as you are in the Top 20 for brand values, it is deemed a success in Brady's eyes.

In fact the West Ham hierarchy are so proud of themselves that they are going to produce a film called Iron Men to commemorate the move. This sounds like it could rival United Passions (see Introduction) as a most fitting tribute to football's infinite capacity for vaingloriousness. What they seem to have completely overlooked are the teething problems that have beset the move. Why allow the odd fight, multiple ejections from the ground and a simmering resentment amongst the majority of fans to get in the way of a good old branding exercise?

But perhaps the last word on this deeply worrying aspect of football should rest with Bolton Wanderers and their association with 188Bet, which lasted for a few years from 2009. The Trotters are not unusual in picking a gambling company as a sponsor although considering the vast damage gambling addiction has had on many footballers' lives it is a tad surprising that they are quite so keen to jump into bed with them. After all every major club has either had a sports betting company as a main sponsor or as an official betting partner, but none have gone quite so far as Bolton.

In the spirit of providing an all-encompassing partnership no doubt 188Bet started to offer live betting on Bolton's youth and Academy teams' matches. Cue moral outrage, including Gordon Taylor, PFA chief executive, who started his playing career at Bolton in 1962. "Youngsters and gambling is a bad mix, and an unhealthy one," Taylor said and let's face it, he should know as in August 2013 there were reports that he reputedly racked up gambling debts of £100,000 to a single bookmaker after a betting spree where he bet £4 million over the space of thirty months.

Bolton have clearly learned their lesson and even though they signed a deal with spinandwin.com for 2016/17 season they drew the line on the sponsor appearing on children's and infants' shirts as "children should not be directly exposed to advertising from betting and gambling companies." Quite right too although what said youngsters are supposed to do when they go to watch the first team in shirts emblazoned with the winandspin.com logo is anyone's guess.

Then we have the full, unexpurgated horror of extending the brand that ends in swallowing up the name of the stadium. Take Cheltenham Town who decided in July 2015 it would be a great idea to change their ground's name from the rather unimposing but simple Whaddon Road to the World of Smile Stadium. The World of Smile Stadium, honestly can you think of a shoddier name than that? For the uninitiated the World of Smile is a conservatories and furniture company based in Cheltenham and this is what their managing director said about the deal.

"You can't say the name World of Smile without grinning and that's what our company is all about: making customers and clients happy with a positive outlook and that is why we are reaching out into the community."

His name is Jon Burke and the fact that this sponsorship deal started just after Cheltenham had been relegated from the Football League was wholly appropriate. After that chastening experience to enter the World of Smile Stadium must have given all the supporters a massive lift and left them wreathed in smiles.

This three-year deal lasted just the one as they returned as champions of the National League the following year. That success seemed slightly tainted by the name change. With the ground soon luxuriating under the title of LCI Rail Stadium, who as we all know are market experts in rail engineering, things are back on the even keel of a prosaically named ground after the touchy feely nightmare of the World of Smile.

Such misguided and inappropriate behaviour is not restricted to these shores as the growth of the brand over the heart and soul of the club becomes more and more prevalent. In the Daily Telegraph Jonathan Liew wrote a withering piece about the "Madridification" of Barcelona, as close to the biggest insult you can possibly imagine to the club that has been the symbol of Catalan independence for so long. Liew argues in the piece that the motto of 'Mes Que un Club' has been systematically gutted and now lies discarded in the headlong rush for commercial supremacy.

Liew does not pull any punches: "Barcelona, the football club built by Joan Gamper at the start of the 20th century as an expression of Catalan regional identity, is now a global brand being leveraged for purposes that are only tangentially connected with football." Such a shift in priorities is an inevitable cause of the current president Josep Bartolomeu's key objective of becoming the first club to exceed €1bn in revenue, football matters almost a sideshow to the main event of financial supremacy.

Finally, a warning from America about how this sort of situation can quickly get out of hand. The Chicago White Sox stadium has been renamed the Guaranteed Rate Field. This is where naming rights takes us to and it is certainly not pretty or indeed acceptable. So let's stop the rot now before it gets too late and we all end up going to the equivalent of the Guaranteed Rate Field for our many and varied sins.

Branding is of course all-pervasive and nothing is quite as ludicrous as some of the personal endorsements that the players get involved in. Take the most famous player on the planet. Cristiano Ronaldo has a dizzying array of products that want to be associated with him, including a blanket. This is not just any old blanket, but one with CR7 emblazoned across it in letters large enough to cause a nosebleed in garishly bright red and green. What it lacks in subtlety it certainly makes up for in sheer unadulterated arrogance. It is quite a feat to believe in yourself so much that you can envisage a time where a blanket is something that you would make it part of your personal portfolio.

CHECKATRADE TROPHY

We've always committed to review the competition and its objectives with our 48 League One and League Two clubs. We said we would do this after the one-year pilot and it will take place in April. We will see if amendments need to be made to the rules for it to continue in this format, whether it continues at all.

Shaun Harvey, Football League chief executive

In terms of uniting football there has been nothing more effective as the Checkatrade Trophy, the latest ruse by the EFL to pass off a sub-standard competition under a suitably underwhelming title. It has been a brilliant way of bringing together fans, players, and managers of every club in a mixture of apathy and condemnation. Nobody likes it and quite frankly they don't care one little jot. The laughably low attendances have underpinned the universal contempt for this half–baked idea and just to put a sprinkling of hundreds and thousands on the massive slice of humble pie served up the EFL decided to dish out fines to a dozen clubs for daring to field slightly less than full strength teams. That's certainly a good way of getting everyone fully behind it.

Of all the furious ripostes to being fined possibly the most admirable was from Bristol Rovers manager, Darrell Clarke: "I've just been trying to get hold of the EFL on the phone to try and find out if they want to pick my team for Saturday. They seem to be calling the shots and I can tell you that I, like many of the other managers who have been punished, am very angry and disappointed. When somebody sat behind a desk with a nice warm cup of coffee can start telling me which first-team players I can and can't play then the game is gone. I wonder if the people who have thought up a ridiculous format that supporters up and down the country have boycotted will think about giving themselves a fine. That's a good question isn't it?"

Yes, Darrell, it is indeed and the question tantalisingly remained unanswered. Perhaps we have got it all wrong and that we are all misguided fools and given time this will gradually turn into a much-loved competition, cherished by all lucky enough to participate. But I am willing to go out on a limb here and suggest that the Checkatrade Trophy or whatever it is going to be called/disguised as will never be a priority in its current shambolic state, nor will it be mourned when it's eventually buried amidst the rubble of rubbish ideas that have been dreamed up by muddle headed administrators.

Let's face it if you wanted to win a popularity contest you would not choose to be heading up any football authority but dear old Shaun Harvey, the EFL chief executive has managed to turn himself into Public Enemy Number 1 with some panache and the Checkatrade Trophy has become a pointed stick with which to beat him around the head. Many critics point out that in a previous life Harvey took three clubs into administration, which is a colourful track record to say the least. One that certainly would have prepared him for pacing up and down the corridors of power wearing an anxious frown.

For a further look into the catastrophic competition that is the Checkatrade Trophy here is Daniel Storey, FSF Football Writer of the Year for 2016, who wrote the following article in November 2016 for Football 365:

"The next stage is getting the group stage under way and the draw has thrown up some exciting prospects. I'm looking forward to seeing how the competition develops on the pitch and also the reaction it gets from the crowd."

If the key to great comedy is timing, the Football League's CEO can look forward to a sell-out stadium tour. Speaking in late-July, Shaun Harvey was proclaiming exactly the sort of 'no no, nothing bad to see here' assessment that has proved so successful in modern politics; perhaps he should be an MP instead?

By every reasonable assessment, the EFL Trophy – let's go with Checkatrade Trophy from now on – has been an abject failure. Having started as the Associate Members' Cup in 1983, becoming the Football League Trophy in 1992, we have now seen the full bastardisation of a competition that once had fine intentions and drew interest from supporters. Never go full bastardisation.

There's a danger of overestimating the importance of the minutiae, but the Twitter handle for the Checkatrade trophy is @Checkatradetrpy, something that becomes even more amusing when you consider that they can't use @Checkatradetrophy because it's too long. The trophy that doesn't even get to spell its own name right on social media; that's quite the PR kick in the balls.

Let's be hyper-generous for a moment. Let's say that Harvey's grand vision, to include Premier League academy teams in the competition, was a well-meaning attempt to give young players more competitive football, and founded on a belief that lower-league fans would be excited by their presence. Let's now be realistic: Everything about that vision was short-sighted.

It started with the immediate rejection of the competition by the teams that mattered most to its success, at least in Harvey's eyes. Arsenal, Liverpool, Manchester United, Manchester City and Tottenham Hotspur all declined to participate, while Newcastle United refused the offer as a Championship club.

The Football League clubs, who had agreed to the proposals partly because they thought it might stem the tide of the 'B teams/League 3' idea but also because the presence of elite clubs did turn the heads of many chairpeople, were left put out. "If I'd have known such a large amount of Premier League sides would not take part then no chance," Peterborough chairman Darragh MacAnthony said.

Others were unconvinced from the start. "We don't feel there would be a benefit even to getting one of the bigger clubs like Manchester United, Manchester City, Liverpool or whoever," said Accrington managing director David Burgess. "Accrington played Manchester United here in the Lancashire Senior Cup here a couple of years ago and there were a few hundred people here. There's no real enthusiasm for under-21s football or reserve-team football or whatever you want to call it."

Even those Premier League clubs who did take part have hardly embraced the competition. Chelsea, Everton, Stoke, West Ham and West Brom were all eliminated with one win between them, leaving Leicester (four points behind Walsall), Swansea (behind AFC Wimbledon), Sunderland (behind Rochdale) and Southampton the only Premier League clubs to qualify.

Of the four FA Youth Cup semi-finalists from last year, Arsenal and Manchester City did not take part while Chelsea and Blackburn might well not have bothered; neither won a game. Even the team names were confused. Some sites list teams as 'Under-21', others as 'Under-23' and others 'reserves and academy' or 'academy'.

Part of the reason for the tournament's failure is a confusing set of rules that promote a message that this is nothing more than glorified reserve-team football. Premier League and Championship sides were forced to name six players in their starting XI who were under 21 at the end of June but senior players still played a prominent role, negating the supposed vision. Teams from Leagues One and Two had to name a minimum of five "first-team" players in the starting XI (with its own detailed definition). It led to ludicrous incidents such as Bradford City goalkeeper Colin Doyle being substituted after 45 seconds of one match.

Anyone surprised that lower-league clubs might react badly to having rules imposed upon them in their own competition might want to reconsider. This is the response to exploitation, by clubs who feel they have been at best ignored and at worst trampled all over.

The result of mistrust and misgivings is disinterest, and the Checkatrade Trophy is at least breaking records in one area. Middlesbrough's home game against Shrewsbury Town was watched by 308 people and 392 watched Fleetwood Town host Blackburn Rovers. Home crowds are regularly measured in the hundreds and away fans in the tens, the reaction to a supposedly regional group draw that produced round trips of up to 340 miles.

'Reports of an away following of 2 at Chesterfield last night are untrue,' Accrington's official Twitter account tweeted. 'We counted at least 6….' *Everyone stands to applause*

Most worrying of all for Harvey is the drop in attendances outside of the fixtures containing Premier League clubs. Cambridge United vs Scunthorpe United drew a crowd of 666, almost three times fewer attendees than Cambridge's game against Dagenham in the first round last year. At Bradford's Valley Parade, 1,865 watched Bury in 2016; 4,127 watched Barnsley last year. At Crewe, 929 attended Chesterfield 2016, while 2,168 watched Wigan in 2015. That suggests that the alterations have not just failed this season, but damaged the entire fabric of the competition moving forward.

Not that Harvey will be deterred from sticking his fingers in his ears and covering his eyes while delivering the party line. Here he is speaking last month: "We need to continue the competition, see what the benefits are and measure it at the end and not at this intervening time. Low crowds are a concern but this was an innovative approach to solve a big problem. We will be doing plenty of work to try and understand what the reticence is towards the competition."

I can help you there, Shaun. Ticket prices for league football are already too high for fans. You then created a regional tournament that ended in ludicrous fixtures. You railroaded clubs into a vote that many presumed was their only way to relieve – or stave off – a more serious concern. You proclaimed the benefits for Premier League clubs who, it subsequently turned out, would rather manage their own academies through Professional Development Leagues. Is that enough to go at?

No? Okay. Supporters are sick of lower-league football being effectively bribed by their governing body. They're sick of being made to feel that their clubs are puppets to assist a Premier League that already enjoys infinitely more benefits at their expense. They're used to the gap, but sick of it being artificially widened.

For a lower-league fan, football has become a version of Heathcote Williams' poem Autogeddon, in which aliens watch earth from above and assume that cars are the life form and people the fuel, being fed in and spat out at regular intervals. Fans are no longer the life form but the fuel for the Premier League.

The Checkatrade Trophy, with its embarrassing attendances and PR own goals, is not the cause of the problems, but the effect. We've at least found the line past which lower-league supporters are no longer prepared to swallow the bad news and then say thank you for the meal.

Postscript

There will no doubt be some attempt at self-justification by the powers that be based on the worryingly high attendance at the Checkatrade Trophy Final between Coventry City and Oxford United. That this charade of a competition somehow managed to attract an extraordinary 74,434 hardy souls to Wembley Stadium should not be allowed to disguise the paltry attendances of this unpopular and divisive tournament. The majority of those were Sky Blues, who have been led a not so merry dance by their owners (SISU) who had ignominiously shunted the club from their home ground to Northampton Town's County Ground, and then after their return to the Ricoh Arena ended up shunting the club down to League Two and their lowest position in almost sixty years. One could forgive the Coventry fans for enjoying their day in the sun when they have had to put up with a massive shitstorm that has enveloped their club over the last decade since SISU took over in 2007.

DESIGNATED SINGING SECTIONS

At this moment it's difficult for us to play at home though, because it is like we are playing in an empty stadium. I was today looking around and it was empty, but not in terms of people because it was obviously full. That's what is frustrating.

Jose Mourinho after Chelsea beat QPR in November 2014

It was not just Mourinho who has found that the atmosphere in Premier League stadiums has moved away from the raucous and ended up drifting into the somnolent. The man who eventually succeeded him as the permanent manager at Stamford Bridge, the irrepressible Antonio Conte, has shown his frustration at the apathy that has now become the norm. Conte has attempted to whip up the crowd from its slumbers and he must be confused by all the reports of how English crowds are the loudest or the most passionate in the world. The Italian exhibits more energy on the touchline than most of the 40,000-odd fans at the home of the 2016/17 Champions. If they showed an ounce of the passion of their manager it would improve the noise levels immeasurably. But some bright spark has come up with a solution of sorts.

If there was ever any need for evidence that football had reached the end of its natural life then the creation of designated singing sections makes it an open and shut case. It is not feasible to be calm about such an idea, the only response is to release the demons and swamp the air with them because this really cannot happen. Just think about this for a second.

Designated.

Singing.

Section.

Everywhere you look this is one seriously bad idea. To have anything designated is anathema to the soul and spirit of football as it is all too deliberate, leaving no room for spontaneity. Singing is not an activity that is suited to the false constraints of a section. They have designated singing sections in churches and cathedrals that are also known as choirs. That is where they should remain.

There is no longer that wall of noise that used to roll down off the terraces and engulf the action with a swathe of the spectators carried away on a tide of emotion. We have now reached the point that there are matches when the only sound that can be heard is that of the players' calls and the managers' exhortations. You simply cannot decree that there are only certain parts of the ground where singing should take place. If this was happening in North Korea we would all be up in arms about such a ludicrous attempt to control people, but this is not Pyongyang it is actually happening in Manchester, Birmingham, London etc. So one wonders what happens to people who start singing outside the designated section. Maybe they are shuffled away and join the list of disappeared. Any resistance is futile and will be met with the firmest of actions. You have been warned.

It was bad enough that Old Trafford, a former cauldron of noise and one that used to intimidate opposition was one of the first grounds to opt for such a scheme. But that pales into insignificance when it was revealed that it was the fans themselves who were behind it. The supporters that congregated in the Stretford End apparently complained to the club that they could not be heard in other parts of the ground. Dale O'Donnell, who is the man behind fans' website Stretty News was quoted in The Daily Telegraph as saying that "the atmosphere for some home games can resemble a library and we want to change that."

Well there is a simple answer to that problem and it does not involve designated singing sections, it revolves around an idea that may be a little ahead of its time but is at least, simple to understand and even simpler to carry out. Just sing louder. If you really see the solution as grouping the most vocal of your supporters in one particular place then I would suggest you have more of a fundamental issue on your hands than merely seating arrangements. It could be time for a transfer, not of players, but of your fans, so that they can go and watch a more appropriate game such as Crown Green Bowls or catch a spot of dressage.

Prior to this revolutionary move, Manchester United revealed in 2013 that they had reached a point of no return in their search for a solution and went as far as employing an acoustics expert to help with the atmosphere. Said acoustics engineer was to report back on his findings but there was a deathly silence and perhaps he succumbed to the dearth of atmosphere. It does seem quite a feat for 75,000 people to be so quiet, maybe they are all choking on their Roy Keane-branded prawn sandwiches.

Questions need to be asked at the very highest level including who dreamed up this ridiculous concept of designated singing sections in the first place, which clubs are seriously considering introducing these crazy ideas and who is going to voluntarily sit in said sections? The idea maybe is better suited to herding of cattle as they generally do not have too much of a say in where they end up. But football fans should resist such a move and make their clubs aware that this is not acceptable on any level. The fear is that this will spread far and wide across the country unchecked and before we know it there will be designated clapping sections, or even designated talking sections.

If clubs do go down this route and introduce these sections maybe they should go the whole hog and hand out lyrics for the best club songs, maybe even provide added instruments to jolly the whole thing along. With the clashing of cymbals and the banging of the odd drum we may even get to hear them above the generic malaise which has engulfed the stadium. Maybe there should even be a series of rehearsals so that the designated singers are up to scratch and singing from the same hymn sheet. If this feels a little far-fetched then just bear in mind that Hull City have alighted on an idea that may well be the perfect accompaniment for such sections by putting the words to chants on the rolling hoardings facing the crowd. So handy for any punters who could not make the rehearsal time and whoever get a little lost in singing along to one of their club's popular anthems. Those who rail at the pampering and spoonfeeding of the current crowds have plenty of ammunition for their argument right there.

This is not too far from another grotesque idea, which has been tried before to the eternal shame of those who perpetrated it. There have been occasions where clubs have piped the noise of a roaring crowd into the stadiums as they could not rely on their fans to generate enough noise. Chelsea seriously considered doing so at Stamford Bridge a few years back as they were concerned about the lack of vocal support for the team. Most recently, West Ham were accused of doing so to try to inject some atmosphere into their soulless bowl of a new home, The London Stadium. The club denied this was true but there were plenty more who testified that this was indeed the case during some of the early games. Maybe this was an attempt to drown out the disgruntled punters voicing their opinions on the football on display or having an issue with not being allowed to stand by over-zealous stewards.

Perhaps a sneaky peek into the future might see all grounds split up into designated noisy and less noisy zones, in a similar way to the quiet coaches on trains, whereby anybody raising their voice above a whisper is removed from the stands. The fact that Manchester United announced a major sponsorship deal with a mattress company offers a glimpse into the future whereby all fans are provided with the necessary equipment for a nice snooze. As the Do Not Disturb signs are put up all over Old Trafford and the rest of the country's leading stadia we can all rest easy in our beds. Welcome to the Theatre of Dreams.

ENCROACHMENT AT THROW-INS

At the moment of delivering the ball, the thrower must throw the ball with both hands over the head from the point where it left the field of play.

FIFA Rules of Football

Of all the rules in football this has to be amongst the simplest to oversee and yet it is transgressed countless times in every match. This could be viewed as a little niche and small beer by comparison to other more important categories, but this is probably the one that happens more often than any other indiscretion and sends me wild without fail. Considering the hoo-ha made about the invisible spray at free kicks it is amazing that at literally every throw-in there are massive liberties taken as to their location. As a side issue the cheering that used to accompany each use of the vanishing spray when first introduced to English football was a blight. The hoopla that accompanied the introduction of vanishing spray covered up the larceny that has continued unabated for years now, but enough of that.

Encroachment is not just about sneaking a couple of yards here and there. This is a massive land grab involving huge chunks of territory, almost so blatant that nobody can quite bring themselves round to correcting it. It has become a nonsensical rule as it is never enforced so maybe the best way of dealing with this is to allow the player taking the throw-in to have five seconds to rush up the touchline before releasing the ball. He probably would not get as far as he does now so surely it is worth consideration.

The next game you watch check out just how the scenario plays out every single time without fail. The ball goes out of play and the player collects it and edges a few yards up the pitch, the ever-alert referee then holds his hand up as if to say that is far enough despite the fact that it is at least five yards from where it should be taken. The player then edges forward ever so subtly hoping the referee will not notice and on the odd occasion that they do they usher the player back. He duly retreats about half the distance he has already stolen and then waits for the ref to approve. Having gained his approval he then prepares finally to take the throw-in and creeps ever so stealthily beyond where he was told to take it from, thus negating the whole charade of having been told to retreat.

One has to question what the assistant referee is up to during this particular charade, as surely his job should be to police such things on his touchline. It never happens as they adopt a laissez faire approach that borders on anarchy. The match officials are often as adjacent as anyone could be when the throw-in is in their half of the pitch but this still does not prevent the temporary blindness that seems to afflict them. Never chastising or correcting a player from stealing at least ten yards is a serious dereliction of duty on their behalf. If one was to aggregate the number of yards stolen in this brazen manner it would likely stretch halfway around the world.

It is not as if they have a lot on their plate in this moment as the ball is dead. There are no offsides to worry about and they could actually concentrate on the one single job in hand, but no this is allowed to go on without any intervention. So one has to wonder what is going through their minds. The fact that it is so blatant makes their inaction doubly reprehensible. Why not just concentrate for a little while on the only job you have and help us rid the game of this infernal nonsense. Just try it once in a while and you never know the players may stop doing it.

And you never know they may start to respect you a little more rather than treating you as little more than a minor inconvenience. Alternatively maybe assistants should be allowed their own can of vanishing spray so they can mark their territory therefore making it easier to spot the perpetrators. This may not be an indiscretion on a grand scale but it is still intensely annoying and it is cheating that is being allowed to continue. So let's call a halt to this as soon as possible. As the Video Assistant Referee is being steadily introduced throughout the game is it not too much to ask that somebody monitors this continuous contravention of the rules?

 THE ENGLAND BAND

There had been a fear before kick-off that 18,000 or so Poles would out-sing and out-atmosphere the home support, albeit anything that might drown out the England band, whose parpings and whumpings tend to produce the feeling of being very slowly lulled into semi-consciousness by a dementedly patriotic stage hypnotist, is to be welcomed.

Barney Ronay in The Guardian on the England Poland World Cup qualifier in 2013

It is difficult to find anybody who would stand up to support the existence of the England Band. Football has not copied many ideas from cricket and after this absolutely diabolical import it is not hard to see why. The Barmy Army have long since annoyed the hell out of anyone who just wanted to watch cricket but now their football equivalent are plaguing Wembley and elsewhere with their infernal racket. Amazingly this has now been going on for the best part of two decades. The idea was taken up by some misguided Sheffield Wednesday fans who were encouraged by the then Wednesday manager, Trevor Francis, to get the band together. Maybe Francis' reputation as the first £1 million footballer needs to be rewritten.

Then the disease spread to the international team. Having started in those heady days post-Euro 96 when they were begrudgingly accepted as some sort of novelty act and we were all swept away on a wave of national euphoria. But they have now been allowed to ruin the lives of thousands of fans for far too long and it is time to call a halt to all their nonsense. If anything symbolised the decline and sorry state that the English national team has experienced over the last five decades then the England Band would be right up at the front of the queue as all other scampered for cover from their infernal forced jollity. Watching England struggle at tournament after tournament is a difficult enough experience as is, the last thing we need is these jolly japesters blasting out their inappropriately merry tunes. It is akin to having an oompah troupe playing at a solemn funeral. We should be allowed to wallow in our misery without the intervention of a frigging brass band.

Why anyone should have to put up with this is beyond me. It is not just that it's intensely annoying but also the fact that they have only learned a couple of tunes over this length of time. Whatever happened to variety or imagination? If I hear the Great Escape song once more I swear I am going to get that man's trumpet and ram it so far down his throat that he is going to have to brush his teeth through an orifice lower than his mouth. When people are stopped from taking bottles of water into grounds how come this lot can take in their instruments, which double up as offensive weapons on a couple of levels. The stewards should be instructed to take them out both metaphorically and literally. Whoever sanctioned this needs to be grilled in front of a public committee and paraded through the streets and into the stocks.

Aside from the repetitive monotony there is also a massive issue with the relevance of this song. The whole premise of the Great Escape film is centred on the triumph of persistence and an against the odds victory. There is a bunch of hard-working heroes who make the most out of limited resources, which is pretty much the reverse of what England have been doing for a while. Now I may have missed something but over the last five decades or so when did the England team do anything remotely heroic? We have been force fed a diet of generally serene qualification against the might of San Marino and Scotland and then the trouble starts as we limp through the group stage of the Finals or not as the case may be. Then reality dawns once again when we meet any opposition of any calibre, such as Iceland, and then that is that. This is nothing to do with the ethos of the Great Escape, if there were an equivalent of the Massive Disappointment that would be more apposite, but maybe that would be a little more difficult to set to music.

This not so merry band even concocted what is laughably called a song for the 2014 World Cup that beggared belief. As we are all acutely aware there have been some pretty ropey football songs in the past but this one really plumbs new depths. If you have never heard it then consider yourself extremely lucky and keep it that way. All I need to tell you is that Bernie Clifton was involved and it was called This Is The Big One. Even if this were semi-ironic it does not really excuse this being foisted on the poor, unsuspecting public. It makes Vindaloo look like a masterpiece of subtle composition and lyrical brilliance by comparison.

EVERY OTHER TEAM

Die: die for adultery! No:
The wren goes to't, and the small gilded fly
Does lecher in my sight.
Let copulation thrive.

"King Lear" act 4, sc. 6,

Writer, comedian and Palace fan Kevin Day contributed to The A-Z of Football Hates and he is back for more. In this most welcome return he turns his ire on those people who keep a second team tucked up their sleeves just in case their first choice turns out to be a dud. It goes against every principle of football support to have such a contingency plan as Kevin explains. And William Shakespeare no less clearly agrees with Kevin if the withering quote from King Lear is anything to go by.

All football fans - and I'm talking proper football fans here, not the sort of fan who lives in Devon, supports Liverpool and spends his evenings trying to get on radio phone-ins - all football fans harbour minor grudges that would seem irrational to people who don't understand the sport.

They may chunter about half and half scarves (the wearing of which by people over the age of six should be a criminal offence); they may be convinced that a particular referee hates their team (yes, you, Mark Clattenburg); they may object to the price of replica shirts (and if anyone can explain to me why any club anywhere needs a third kit I'd be grateful).

Every football fan will definitely have a list of teams they dislike for one reason or another: whether it's because they are local rivals, or because they once stole a favourite player, or simply because they have a habit of winning big games against you.

I take things more seriously than that, which is why picking a letter in the A to Z of football niggles was very easy for me...it's E which stands for 'Every other club in the country'.

I am completely baffled when I meet somebody at a wedding and they say: "Oh, I support Tottenham but my second team is Orient and I always look out for Oxford United's scores because I went to university there".

Within seconds of meeting them I already hate them because they support Spurs, they have a second team, and they went to Oxford. It's why I don't get invited to weddings any more.

For me, having a passionate obsession for Crystal Palace is only matched by my passionate dislike of the 91 other clubs in the country. It's a source of great regret to me that they can't all lose every week.

It's a given that I hate Brighton, but I also hate all other football fans for not hating them. How any intelligent, morally aware football fan cannot instinctively hate them from birth is a complete mystery to me.

But I also seriously dislike every other team as well.

Sometimes for a reason: like having a brick thrown at me at Luton, or the train back from an evening game at Blackburn breaking down, or burning my tongue on a pie at Sheffield United, but I don't need a reason - I mostly hate them because they are not Palace.

And, by the way, if you're thinking that there's no logic to that then you are reading the wrong book. Of course there's no logic to it, it's football that's one of the reasons it's the only true sport in the world.

When my son was eight he came up to me very solemnly as I came back from Selhurst Park on a Saturday evening. "Dad", he said. "Can I support Chesterfield?"

"Of course son", I said, "providing you pack your bags and leave the house now, then you can support who you want. But leave the Palace duvet on your bed for the child I adopt to replace you."

After Mrs. Day had calmed him down and threatened to hit me with my Palace garden gnome, I asked him why Chesterfield?

He said "well, dad, you never come home from football happy and I don't want that all my life so I've decided to support another team. I got all the way down to Chesterfield before I found a team that I've never heard you say you hate".

Bless him. I pointed out that happiness is not the point of football, - quite the opposite in fact - but clever lad that he was, the philosophical implications evaded him a bit.

So, instead I pointed out that I did hate Chesterfield (and I do, I can't stand the way they go on about that bleeding crooked spire on their church. If the only thing you've got going for your team is that you can see a bent building from the ground, then you need to find another team. But then I'd hate them even more for swapping allegiances so they can't win).

Then I explained to my son that he was going to have to look a long way down the non-league tables before he found a team that I didn't actively dislike and the chances were they wouldn't have a nice, warm club duvet that he could snuggle under to drown out the sound of daddy shouting at Match of the Day.

I'm glad to say that story has a happy ending. My son is now a fully functioning Palace fan who only snuggles under the duvet to watch dodgy internet feeds of away games. And, he hates Brighton even more than I do. I'm a very proud man.

Postscript

It is worth noting that Kevin's words of wisdom will resonate across the land and particularly within my household as all three of my children have been inculcated with the need to detest Brighton and its Hove Albion. However, the publisher of this book, Dave Hartrick, is by some strange twist of fate a bloody Seagull and of course they have finally managed to reach the Premier League for the first time in their sorry history. As the 2017/18 season shimmers in the near distance the enmity is about to get serious.

FANBOYS - THE RISE OF THE

A boy or man who is an extremely or overly enthusiastic fan of someone or something.

Definition of fanboy from the Merriam-Webster dictionary

Stephen Tudor, aka The Daisy Cutter, is a blogger, freelance writer and a Manchester City fan. Here Tudor bemoans the tedious nature of social media's obsession with the endless comparisons between two of the greatest players to have graced the football pitch. The Argentinean and the Portuguese have shared FIFA's Ballon d'Or between them like brothers fighting over a favourite toy. To reduce the rivalry between two of the finest exponents of the game to some childish spats over the Internet is a crying shame, and one that has certainly got to Tudor.

In the feisty relationship between social media and football there's ample reason to look to the skies and quietly wish for an apocalypse.

Just a few minutes spent on any Facebook supporter's group page following a poor performance is sufficient to worry the spleen and weep for mankind. The best player must immediately be flogged for a pittance. The manager should be given his P45 then reinstated just so he can be sacked again. It's like Mumsnet on ketamine. A competition of stupid. I believe the collective term for these people is a jerk of knees.

Over on Twitter the deluded sense of entitlement from anyone allied with a Premier League club would be unsavoury were it not ball-achingly funny. Liverpool supporters – whose side have qualified for the Champions League once in the previous six seasons [now twice in seven season after 2016/17's noble fourth place] – get all uppity when Lovren, Can and Firmino bafflingly fail to replicate the imperious standards set by Hansen, Case and Dalglish while Gooners – whose side's trophy haul for a generation amounts to three FA Cups – lambast Wenger for not signing the world's elite. Strangely they often choose to go elsewhere to enjoy the thrill of lifting silverware.

At times stumbling upon a reasoned tweet on your timeline feels like finding a raft in an ocean of ignorance and juvenile vines. You cling to it. You read it twice. Elsewhere we're awash with fickle bellendery as insecure individuals with keyboards for megaphones vie for attention with hyper-inflated opinion. These people procreate; they converse and interact with the sane. And that is genuinely quite troubling.

Yet all this amounts to an irritating itch in comparison to the virtual measles that spreads across the face of social media after any Barcelona, Real Madrid, Argentina or Portugal competitive fixture. Ladies and gents we are living in the age of the fanboy. All hail the rise of the modern idiot. Raised on Sky montages set to Vangelis these over-excited pimply virgins care little for the unfathomable matrix of chaos and disappointment that is football while a well-organised stalemate is anathema to them: All that matters is the over-the-top celebration of two of its finest exponents Ronaldo and Messi.

At this point I should state the bleeding obvious. Both are supernaturally brilliant. Freakishly good. We are all extremely fortunate to have the game's Beatles and Stones both riding high in the charts in our lifetime. Unfortunately their online cheerleaders – of which there are legions – have the knicker-wetting excitability of One Directioners.

So don't follow them I hear you cry. Well I don't natch. Yet through retweet after retweet they permeate my timeline with their infantile vines, memes and excessive declarations of genius absolutely always committed in capital letters and vomited liberally with emojis. Honestly they are harder to avoid than Josh Widdicombe.

Each weekend evening in particular it is, to use a term that may or may not exist but sounds suitably yoofy, a Twitter takedown. Then there are the stats. Lots and lots of stats. That was Messi's 7500th goal in 500 La Liga games. Ronaldo's hat-trick was his 50th in 49 games, breaking an 80 year record of logic and physics. They are legend. He is genius. They're just too good.

God bless their childish enthusiasm but each week feels like a religious sect has edited Match magazine and let themselves into my house to beat me repeatedly about the head with a copy. Yet it gets worse. Much, much worse. Because these children of the damned are not united in their adoration and propaganda. They cannot share the belief that we are truly blessed to witness first-hand these two phenomenal talents in the same era and be done with it. One must be better than the other. I mean, you can't listen to Sgt Pepper and Let It Bleed back-to-back. That would just be madness.

This debate – oh sweet baby Jesus this dreary, dreary debate – rages on, ramping up their hyperbole to the utterly ridiculous and obliterating any semblance of reason or calm analysis it might otherwise contain. Messi is sick. Ronaldo out of this world. Messi sucks. Ronaldo has skillz. It's internet daubing onto a pencil case.

Who do I think is better? I think I had an opinion on this some time ago but stopped caring around 2012 and lost the will to live shortly after. It would be very nice to use social media at some point in the near future without feeling like I am being accosted by a multitude of teenage Hare Krishnas at an airport but alas I see no end in sight.

We are living in the age of the fanboy. All hail the rise of the idiot.

Next year we can win the quadruple.

Ty, Arsenal Fan TV

When Robbie and Ty popped up on Match of the Day's coverage of the 2017 FA Cup Final many people felt that this was the moment that Arsenal Fan TV had jumped the shark. Having previously been the ever so slightly subversive voice of the under-represented common or garden supporter the exposure on the most mainstream of football broadcasts marked the end for many. Here Seb Stafford-Bloor runs the rule over the phenomenon of Fan Channels from Set Pieces Pieces of Hate back in November 2015. Stafford-Bloor is a freelance writer who writes regularly for FourFourTwo and is content editor at uMAXit.

Fan channels are popular in 2015 and it's not hard to understand why. This is now a world in which the supporter feels marginalised and so it's entirely natural for a movement which returns their voice be embraced. If the modern day fan has really just become a consumer, then social media - despite its many evils - does at least add a pair of eyes to the corporate facade.

They are a force for good, then. They allow supporters to be heard at a time when clubs are only interested in holding them by their ankles and shaking their pockets empty. Catching fans immediately after they leave matches, these cameras capture that elusive real-person angle that Sky and BT seem less than interested in and present a perspective which challenges Richard Scudamore's perfect world.

They are an excellent idea. Twitter may have provided a stage for everyone to dance and shout on, but fan channels have added a third dimension. Real people, real faces; it works because it conveys emotion by a means other than block capitals, exclamation marks and irate emojis.

Well, in the beginning it did. Now, as the genre evolves, that original concept is mutating into something ugly. Rather than being a true depiction of fan culture, they reward those with the loudest voices and the lowest levels of self-respect. Less forums of self-expression and more avenues for low-grade opportunity, they are becoming character creation factories. The ubiquitous Arsenal Fan TV, for instance, has become a theatre of the absurd in which preposterously affected personalities are thrust into the football community's conscious. It's all scripted buzz-phrases and Jeremy Kyle culture and it possesses the charm of watching two unpopular children being forced to fight in a playground.

There's Claude (angry, middle-aged) pointing and shouting at Ty (merchandise fetish), there are the smirking faces behind them giving knowing looks to the camera, and here we all are laughing away at this humanity car-crash - and we aren't just slowing down to see the accident, we're getting out of the car, setting up deckchairs and gathering around the wreckage.

It's The Only Way is Essex or Made In Chelsea, just without any of the make-up, music, or reassuring knowledge that everyone reverts to relative normality when the ad breaks roll. These characters may have refined their catchphrases and practiced their rants in the bathroom mirror, but they are almost exclusively the object of the humour rather than an actual part of it.

While it may be pious to insist that all fan channels should exist exclusively with a straight-face, it's still dispiriting to watch the industry break its ideological moorings and drift into questionable waters. It's become an exploitative mocku-soap in which the more times Bully (Nose ring) can make Mo ("net spend") cry the better.

And as the online traffic surges, so does the temptation to bend to that demand.

Like the well-intentioned circus owner who has watched the crowds tire of his acrobats, jugglers and elephants, the cheap heat of freak show voyeurism has been allowed to subvert this industry's honesty. The views are up and the revenue is rolling in, and the temptation to keep pushing the three-nosed curiosities into the spotlight grows ever more overwhelming.

But for all of Arsenal Fan TV's unsettling melodrama, a more potent evil is starting to flow through the industry's veins.

Like any developing market place, this genre's success and its increasing value has attracted outsiders. While many who were present at the industry's birth still retain an independent quality - and an authentic, mouth-piece function - the dark hand of professionalism can be felt elsewhere. The original entrepreneurs may have struck oil with a bucket and spade, but now the heavy duty rigs are being craned onto the fertile ground.

SpurredOn, Full Time Devils, Chelsea Fans' Channel and Blue Moon Rising are all operated by Shotglass Media, a digital wing of Fremantle UK, the production company behind The Apprentice, Take Me Out and Britain's Got Talent. Big budget backing discredits the "by the fans, for the fans" selling-point, because it implies the existence of a business decision and a cost/benefit analysis. These channels aren't being set-up by supporters who suffer the game's peaks and troughs, but by hair-gelled suits who are after a quick fondle of football's gusset.

"Hey, what's up guys! Isn't Emmanuel Adebayor a lazy money-grabber?"

Close your eyes and you can almost hear the brainstorm: who do the fans hate? What are their engagement rates like for this topic? Which demographics are we targeting here?

It's all faux-passion and forcefully slurred vowels; it's you and I, but after we've spent a year at RADA and been dressed in the latest derelicte collection. Trained, stylised presenters artfully dip topics in outrage-kerosine, hold them against social media's perpetual flame, and wait for the fires of digital revenue to burn. Part of the cold set of capitalist realities though it may be, it is also symptomatic of a particularly toxic cynicism. A supporter's passion is personal and this is really just a clandestine way of taxing it.

The industry's founding fathers are to be applauded for identifying a niche and forgiven for breeding something which has grown beyond their control. But the perimeter has been breached now; invading agencies are inside the building and they are bagging up as much of the game's soul as they can find. Maybe it represents the final frontier of the game's monetisation? The point at which everything a supporter does, thinks or feels can be converted into cash for somebody else.

There was a benevolent purpose to fan channels once and a genuine intention to use them to reclaim something that had been taken. That's still visible in the father and son who talk honestly about the game or the season-ticket holder who's worried about an ageing centre-half, but that layer occurs metres below the pantomimic posturing and the corporate misdirection.

In 1962 the founding fathers of fantasy football created a game that today inspires, infatuates and confounds millions of players. After a seemingly endless night of labor (sic) pains, the discomfort smoothed by a little alcohol for medicinal purposes, the birth of fantasy football finally took place at a hotel in New York City back in the fall (sic) of 1962.

From 1994 edition of "Fantasy Football Index" magazine

Since its birth over 50 years ago Fantasy Football has become ubiquitous; every media outlet be it newspaper, website, broadcaster worth their salt runs their own version. In fact nearly every office in the land has one. Back in January 2017, Olly Ricketts, freelance writer, railed against the Colins of this world who indulge in the office variety in one of Set Pieces feature "Pieces of Hate".

As the dust settles on an underwhelming January transfer window, several million fantasy league players will have embraced the spirit of blind panic displayed by many a real-life manager.

The transfer wildcard system allows fans to emulate their favourite bosses by ripping up their teams and starting again. Harry Redknapp would be proud of those who replaced every single player in a ten-minute burst, while Kenny Dalglish would certainly empathise with anyone who brought in Andy Carroll at great expense because he scored that bicycle kick.

You'll undoubtedly have shared some top banter with people in the office about it. You'll have laughed at Colin in Finance being below you in the table despite how seriously he takes the whole thing, and you'll have rolled your eyes as others claim not to have checked their team since September. It's all clean, harmless fun – just a bit of a laugh, right? Wrong. Fantasy football is complete and utter bullshit.

The reasons for this are plentiful. Firstly, the excruciating team names. Yes, Colin, I do understand that you have made a pun based on the fact that some well-known football teams have the word 'Athletic' in their names whereas you are 55-years-old and weigh 26 stone. It's truly excellent stuff, it really is. And yes Colin, I realise I am perhaps taking things too seriously by openly seething at the fact that your team is so unbalanced as to be guaranteed relegation were it to play in real life. But I really cannot agree with you playing four left-backs and no defensive midfielders. It is beyond fantasy.

Similarly, I must take issue with your choice of Diego Costa as captain, in spite of his most recent example of inspirational leadership, which saw him agitate for a move to China. This is not some sort of reverse psychology masterstroke – he gets double points and therefore represents another fundamental flaw in a game, which bears no resemblance to the sport on which it is based. And no, Colin, it is not your fault it is usually far better to have an average Arsenal player in your side than an exceptional Sunderland one, were such a thing to exist. Don't hate the player, hate the game, as they say. I do, Colin, believe me I do.

Which reminds me, you support Manchester United, so why were you so eager to tell me you have Kevin De Bruyne and Sergio

Aguero in your team. Shouldn't you wish nothing but harm on them? Is it because each year there is a pool of players without whom you simply cannot do well and, rather than take the honourable route and not pick them, your fear of missing out leads you to cheer for your most hated rivals?

One year I recall that if you didn't have Marcus Gayle, you really weren't going to get very far. Marcus. Gayle. On this point alone I would be within my rights to smugly state that 'I have no further questions your honour' and get off my Pieces of Hate soap box, a landmark case assured in spite of the fact that this wasn't actually a question and we are not actually in court.

But there's more. The cast iron, indisputable proof that fantasy football is a stupid game is as follows: My dad, who knew absolutely nothing about football, came 12th in the Daily Telegraph's Euro 2004 fantasy league. At one point he was as high as eighth, and in with a realistic chance of winning serious money.

While my studiously researched, perfectly balanced side laboured in 120,000th place, my dad's team – which consisted of Milan Baros (whom he got mixed up with Djibril Cisse, naturally), Zinedine Zidane (whose surname he insisted on pronouncing Zyedayne in spite of ample evidence to the contrary), plus nine randoms that he couldn't pick out of a line-up (and as the horror unfolded I really did put one together and put it to the test) – swept aside all before them.

His tactics extended little further than picking some expensive players he had heard of (and as we have established, he didn't even get that right) and then padding the side out with a load of cheap blokes from Greece. Oh how I laughed at his folly, as I finished my marathon scouting session of talented unknowns from the likes of Croatia, Italy and Germany. If fantasy football rewarded knowledge of the game and tactical insight, I was a shoo-in. I forgot one important detail: fantasy football does not reward knowledge of the game and tactical insight. It is a rubbish game that rewards idiots.

My dad died last year, so I will now never get the chance to exact revenge (not that I'd want to, as I think I've made perfectly clear I am in no way bitter and I don't even care). You might expect my first piece of football-related writing since then to focus on all the times he watched my youth games on his one morning off as I hopelessly flailed about the pitch. Or that I would express my gratitude for all the times he drove me the 190-odd miles from home to Anfield so I could watch the likes of Bjorn Tore Kvarme and Salif Diao flail about the pitch.

But I am distinctly comfortable with instead using this opportunity to summarily discredit his one football-related achievement; he would, after all, expect nothing less. So screw you, fantasy football.

They should send details of the flag with the appropriate fire certificate to m.brindle@arsenal.co.uk at least 10 working days before the game. We will then consult with Stadium Management and a decision will be made from there.

Part of Arsenal's official response to FSF's request to all clubs about whether fans could bring flags to the ground from December 2015

The idea of showing loyalty to your club can be displayed in many ways and bringing a flag into a ground should be a relatively straightforward process but judging by Arsenal's response above (which was incidentally only one of five guidelines) there is more to it than meets the eye. It almost seems as though the club is making it as difficult as possible to do so. Do not cross swords with Stadium Management whatever you do.

The Premier League's position as the richest in the world has remained pretty insurmountable over the last decade or so. The grounds are generally packed (attendance levels for 2016/17 season stood at an impressive 95% if figures are to be believed, only three clubs reported attendances under 90% - West Brom, Hull City, and, of course, Sunderland) but many complain with some justification that the atmosphere within the grounds has diminished and the library culture has taken over. Anyone raising the idea of bringing an uncertified flag is frowned upon and if you have the temerity to stand up during a passage of play then you risk expulsion from the ground and the possibility that your library card may well be removed.

There is no doubt that English football at the highest level has become more sanitised and predominantly middle class as admission prices continue to rise, leaving the less well off disenfranchised and the well heeled in charge. No sane person would advocate a return to the troubled times of the 1980s when the threat of hooliganism reared its ugly head on a depressingly regular basis. However, this is not to say that there are not a fair few developments that have been at best ill judged, or at worst are absolute abominations.

When spontaneity is replaced by orchestrated demonstrations the omens are not good and this particular idea is most definitely in the 'not good' category. In a bid no doubt to provide more colour and something verging on the spectacular in the stands some clubs have decided unwisely to utilise massive team flags that are brandished by staff whenever a goal is scored by the home team. And when I say massive I mean massive. And it is not as though the space is well utilised and delivering a meaningful or original message. No they are the bog standard club badges magnified a thousand times, not a particularly imaginative use of space. Their crime would be less heinous if there was something more innovative than the over-sized bloody club crest being shoved in our faces. Somebody should have pointed out to these clubs that size is not everything but then again they are not that keen on the quality over quantity argument or of listening to what fans have to say in the first place.

If you have the misfortune to be seated behind one of these monstrosities then you would be forgiven for hoping against hope that your team never score as you will not be seeing the action on the pitch for a while. If you grow frustrated by the time it takes to stop the swaying and do something radical like stand up, you know the consequences. And so the only options remaining are either to sit in ignorant bliss or continue to watch the game uninterrupted on your handheld device/laptop.

I have nothing against flags per se and own up to having waved the odd one at a Cup Final or two but they have to be of the appropriate scale. I would suggest limiting the size to that of the match programme and no more. When the flag becomes too large to be carried by a small child it has clearly become a nuisance and should be banned from the stands accordingly.

Arsenal and Chelsea are both being named and shamed right here as they have been at this dubious practice for a fair few years now and show no signs of contrition or remorse. The co-perpetrators at the Emirates and Stamford Bridge need to realise that this is not actually achieving anything; in fact the only atmosphere it is creating is one of brooding resentment. It is a major pain in the arse for those in the stadium as has already been mentioned above but maybe the people behind the idea were not too concerned about the poor sods at the game as this is all about how it looks on our screens.

Well I have got some bad news for those great minds who dreamed up this idea. It looks absolutely shit on television as well. Such a display looks completely out of place in a football ground. It is the sort of exhibition you would expect to see at a medieval pageant or at a One Direction gig but not at a football match. The fact that the people responsible for waving the flags clearly are struggling to undertake their task is one thing. Furthermore the whole thing looks so painfully laborious and ungainly that it actually becomes a source of anger and disillusionment amongst those watching at home. It is distracting and irritating in equal measure. So effectively this has alienated both those that attend the games and those that watch on television. A genuine double whammy.

Then of course there are the flag-wavers themselves who must have turned up late to the pre-match meeting and have been consigned to the task that nobody else wants. In the ranking of jobs undertaken by casual staff on match days this one comes quite a long way behind those detailed to pick chewing gum out of the urinals with their teeth. Am not sure what specialist training these poor individuals have to subject themselves to but you can be pretty certain that this is not something that anybody would volunteer for. It must be regarded as some form of draconian punishment for previous misdemeanours. The risk of injury must be dangerously high and the odd dislocated shoulder or torn stomach muscles must all be part of the flag-wavers' lot, alongside the humiliation of having to explain to friends and family exactly what it is they do at the club on a Saturday afternoon. So we are now in the realms of a triple whammy if such a thing existed and if it did not, then it does now.

Flags are not a new concept within football circles and have been favoured by fans particularly in Europe and South America as a way of showing their allegiance. Perhaps the most famous use of a club flag was the rather contentious display by a Scot in Turkey way back in 1996. In his one and only season as the manager of Galatasaray, Graeme Souness would have been acutely aware of the fierce rivalry with Fenerbache. Thus his planting of the Galatasaray flag in the Fenerbache centre circle as a post-match statement at the end of the domestic cup final was certainly lacking in subtlety. This act made some of his more outrageous fouls when he was a combative player look pale and harmless by comparison. It remains a topic of heated debate some twenty years on and provides incontrovertible truth that flags and football really do not mix.

There are other examples of flags in football but none of them make a convincing argument for justifying their presence. There is now an increasing tendency amongst clubs to place tawdry plastic flags on the seats of their fans as if it were a symbol of how much the club values their loyal supporters. It is a hollow gesture that grates rather than bonds so most fans will discard such an item as a piece of tat and consign them to the nearest bin. Along with those bloody clappers, but do not get me started.

Finally, what really bothers me more than anything else is where do they put those ridiculously over-sized bits of canvas when they have finished with them. It's not as though you can tuck them away into the broom cupboard, or pop them into the corner of the dressing room and simply forget about them. I have been racking my brains for the best place to store them and have come up with one suggestion, which may provide a handy solution for us all. Here's a clue to help you - this place is mentioned in a popular, slightly bawdy football chant, it rhymes with glass and would accommodate such material sideways if so required.

FRANCHISE FOOTBALL

This is the most unique story in football, AFC Wimbledon. The story is football, it's for the greater good of football. Every time I talk about this story I go wow; no wonder they want to make a film about it.

Neal Ardley, AFC Wimbledon manager

I have touched on various undesirable elements of the American influence on football but if there is one evil that stands out from the rest it is the idea of franchises taking over our clubs. There have been numerous examples in US sport where dozens of clubs have moved to new locations with barely a thought for the city that is losing their own team. These are leagues that are effectively closed off as they do not entertain the idea of promotion/relegation so this represents the only chance to get a new team into the leagues.

Most moves are primarily motivated by money as the chance to maximise revenue proves too much to resist. This is not a meritocracy where clubs earn the right to participate because of their performances and their quality, as happens here. We used to scoff at such brazenly mercenary behaviour and laugh at their crassness and it was tempting to say that this would never happen here. Now it has come to haunt us and the threat it poses to the fabric of the game is all terribly real.

Talk to any fans of AFC Wimbledon about what happened back in 2003 when their club was unceremoniously ripped from their midst and dumped in Milton Keynes and you will be assailed with howls of protest and more angst than is strictly healthy. Such anger and resentment is fully justified as this is absolutely against the founding principles of English football. The schadenfreude experienced when AFC Wimbledon overtook MK Dons, rising above them in League One in early October 2016 reverberated across the land and was duly celebrated by most right-minded people. It is rare that everybody in football is of one voice but this was one of those occasions. This was one in the eye for those who think that it is acceptable to rip up a century of football history to establish a team rather than build it organically. After only 14 years' existence AFC Wimbledon overtook their nemesis in one of the sweetest moments of retribution since King Charles I lost his head courtesy of Oliver Cromwell and his band of Parliamentarians back in the 1649/50 season.

The heroic efforts of all at AFC Wimbledon should be applauded but let's hope that this will not need to be repeated but if we all thought that this was merely a curiosity and an unpleasant but isolated one-off, the spectre of franchise football reared its ugly head when Red Bull started to show signs of interest in English football. Having started in their native Austria in 2005 with the takeover of SV Austria Salzburg being transformed overnight into the ugly duckling of FC Red Bull Salzburg, they have begun to spread their tentacles far and wide. So naturally there is a New York Red Bulls club as well as South American counterpart, Red Bull Brasil. All these clubs have been founded with budgets that dwarf their peers and have led to a succession of promotions whilst giving rise to their continuing unpopularity amongst the other clubs in their respective countries. The Red Bull logo has become like a red rag to other bulls who they continuously rub up the wrong way.

Not content with having already made their German club Leipzig the most reviled in Europe, they have set their sights on challenging MK Dons' previously unassailable position as the most loathed club in England. The rise of AFC Wimbledon echoes that of RB Leipzig but their approach could not be more diametrically opposed. Whilst the Dons started life in the Combined Counties League, the ninth tier of the English league pyramid as an entirely new club, Red Bull decided to swallow up an existing club in a move not a million miles away from MK Dons. Having taken over a fifth division club called SSV Markranstadt in 2009 and injected huge amounts of cash they have shot up the leagues and duly reached the Bundesliga in 2016. RB Leipzig's existence seems to flaunt the much-revered 50+1 rule, which stipulates that all clubs should be owned by the club's fans or members, as opposed to external investors. At the last count RB had 17, the majority of whom are senior employees of Red Bull, compared to Dortmund and Schalke who each have around 140,000 members. Seemingly RB Leipzig have not got the hang of this rule or maybe they have chosen to ignore it but either way they are considered by most as the 'plastic club'.

The hackles have been well and truly raised amongst German fans as illustrated by one of the more vocal fan groups in Borussia Dortmund who protested against RB Leipzig's presence in the Bundesliga by not attending the away match early in the 2016/17 season. "Of course Dortmund makes money, but we do it in order to play football," said Jan-Henrik Gruszecki, one of the protest organisers in a Guardian interview with Philip Oltermann. "But Leipzig plays football in order to sell a product and a lifestyle. That's the difference."

Cologne fans took even more direct action by barring Leipzig's team coach from getting near to the stadium and delaying the kick-off by 15 minutes whilst at Dynamo Dresden somebody resorted to throwing a severed bull's head on to the pitch. That was certainly an apposite way of exposing this bullshit.

And, of course there are plenty of candidates for Red Bull's ambitions in this country with so many clubs across the divisions struggling financially and with an unhealthy glut of unscrupulous owners who are desperate to get out and cut their losses, this could be a godsend. Think Blackburn Rovers, Charlton Athletic,

Coventry City, Leyton Orient and many, many more. Maybe Hereford FC are in their sights as the catchy idea of christening the club that had to reform back in 2014 after the demise of Hereford United as Red Bull Bulls might appeal to them. To be fair the new Hereford is very much a fan-owned club, having been established by supporters trust so the idea of a takeover would be anathema to the current owners.

Red Bull will not be overly concerned about the fans who quite frankly have been both meddlesome and tiresome in their perpetual protests whilst moaning at the poor running of the club so they deserve little better, is how their warped logic will dictate. The rumours of Red Bull circling around the carcasses of stricken English clubs are bound to grow over the coming years until eventually they snaffle up some poor, unsuspecting club and the latest outpost is conquered by the Red Bull franchise.

It clearly is too much to ask The Football League to step in and consign this idea to the dustbin as in the past the League has stood back and allowed so much to happen without any intervention, this is hardly going to rouse them out of their slumber. With the authorities passive and powerless it will be left to those disenfranchised fans to stand up and be counted once more. Resisting the concept of turning clubs into the sporting equivalent of KFCs or McDonalds is a fundamental concern of all genuine football fans. Although this may be howling against the wind it needs to be done in an attempt to protect our game from further damage and denigration. The FFF - Fighting Franchise Football - could well be the rallying call for a new generation of disillusioned fans as they tackle the evil machinations of the likes of Red Bull and their insatiable expansionism.

———

FREESTYLERS

All you need is a BALL! This is the mantra which all athletes of Freestyle Football have lived by for the past six years. Freestyle Football Federation was formed for two simple reasons; to grow this wonderful sport in all parts of the world and give freestylers a reason to enjoy the movement together.

From the home page of Superball 2017

Now I will not have a word said against the contributor of this piece. Yes, David is a Brighton fan, as we have already discovered, who does indeed live in Yorkshire and yes he does describe himself as a Batman obsessive. But most importantly, he is my publisher, Mr. Ockley Books and you would not have been reading this without his support and guidance.

Before I get into this I think it's worth looking at a couple of lists, the first being things it's important to be able to do if you want to play football at any sort of competitive level:

1. Control a ball
2. Pass a ball over varying distances with any degree of accuracy
3. Shoot reasonably straight
4. Tackle well, know how to physically challenge for space and the ball
5. Dribble over at least ten yards

All fairly simple. Now for another list, this time it's things that you don't need to be able to do if you want to play football at any sort of competitive level:

1. Do a press-up whilst controlling the ball behind your head
2. Remove any item of clothing as you juggle the ball
3. Do ten or more keepie-ups with your shoulder
4. Put it 'top bin' with no pressure, loads of tries, and no goalkeeper
5. Say the word 'tekkers' a lot

You see there's an issue here. Freestyling is to football as Frisbee Golf is to playing the Ryder Cup. There's just no comparison. Yet here we are in a world where freestylers earn thousands of pounds from football fans for doing things really well in circumstances that would never, ever occur in the sport they're making money from. It's a funny old game, Saint.

There is a great deal of skill involved in doing what freestylers do, and I admire them for having the ability to do it, but now the slow drip feed of this stuff is coming into the mainstream and creating a completely wrong ideology for the latest generation of football fans. Allow me to explain.

Last season during a Liverpool game, Sadio Mané nutmegged a West Ham defender but then the ball ran out for a goal kick. Nice bit of skill but ultimately no reward. A few minutes later a short six-second clip appeared on Twitter, the home of rational thought and measured opinion. The ball running out to touch had been left off the end, the nutmeg was the only action along with the words 'Mané's just ended another defender's career lol #lfc'.

What occurred to me was that the end result just wasn't important. The facts the chance had gone, his team mates had run into position for nothing, and he had just handed the ball back to the opposition were all irrelevant. You see he'd done nutmeg, lads, a nutmeg! He'd ended the defender's career, dead of shame and embarrassment, lads! He'd done something so good I'd put my pint of Carling down for a minute and recorded it on the wrong aspect ration on my iPhone, lads! A nutmeg lads! Career over, million hits on YouTube and 500 retweets, lads!

Maybe I am just old fashioned but for me the fact he had wasted the chance to actually create something was more important than the very slight embarrassment he may have caused a defender in doing so. Football is a simple game, there have never been points awarded for style - that's ice-skating you're thinking of. We all love watching a truly great team in their pomp attacking, but not once have I seen a practical application for being able to do five keepie-ups with your heel. Tricks are good when they're practical and they work, putting the ball out for a goal kick not so much.

Freestylers are now big business too, some earning huge contracts from sportswear companies and making decent money from YouTube to boot. Having some experience with youth football I've seen kids do amazing things in the warm up only to then either lack the very basics to be able to play in a game or be ridiculously selfish, trying something showy for the one time in a hundred it comes off and they can shout TEKKERS. Here we are, our failing national team now being managed by Gareth Southgate, unable to move on because our players are technically excellent but tactically thick.

I don't blame freestylers for all of football's ills but this fetishization of irrelevance annoys me at a level I usually reserve only for Nigel Farage. Football is still great, despite everything the product remains lovable and it has done its very best to change that in recent years admittedly. However, around the game the layers of people making money with tenuous links to the actual sport increase - freestylers another symptom of this. What's wrong with, you know, actually playing a game of football?

When Gareth Bale outpaced an entire Internazionale defence both home and away a few years ago he did so with application of speed, an ability to perform one of basics brilliantly, and tunnel vision in terms of getting past his man. Not one of us who watched those wonderful, breathless performances so thrilled for 180 minutes thought to ourselves yeah, but if only he'd done a few more keepie ups. What happens on the pitch in football circumstances matters, what happens on the 47th take on a 4G pitch with no one around and no goalkeeper doesn't.

So freestylers do your thing but don't for a minute think it's got anything to do with football. And kids, watch your Youtube videos all day long and then see how long you can balance the ball on your knee but remember to work on passing a ball accurately over 20 yards too. I know which will make you the better footballer.

———

GOAL MUSIC

**The synergies between football and music could hardly be more apparent or harmonious, with both stirring human emotions across the globe like almost nothing else...
In many countries, the scoring of a goal is marked by a celebratory tune over the stadium PA.**

From FIFA.com

The origins of playing music to celebrate a goal are, like so many of the most pernicious influences in football, straight from the USA. I remember first watching American Football back in the 1980s and there was this perpetual musical accompaniment to every move. As the Hammond organ was cranked up it was almost impossible not to be distracted by the cacophony being belted out. Goal music is akin to the Mexican wave as yet another unwanted import makes its way from across the Atlantic. Apparently back in the 1980s and 1990s, the tune that was the default song of North American Soccer League and its successor Major League Soccer was The Trammps' "Disco Inferno", which in itself is a pretty decent song but not something we need to hear being played every time the home team scores a goal. It should remain as part of the Saturday Night Fever soundtrack and not venture too far from there thanks very much, and most certainly not into a football ground.

I might be a tad biased and could even be accused of losing editorial objectivity here but there is only one goal music that is permitted and that is "Glad All Over". Primarily because it is quite simply the best football song ever that makes all the others pale into insignificance. We even had the band perform the song live on the Selhurst Park pitch back in February 1968. In fact it is so good that other fans have been prone to stealing the song and trying to make it theirs. Man City fans welcomed Pep to the Etihad at the start of the 2016/17 season with their bastardised version of the classic song supplanting the original lines with Guardiola as the catchy chorus. Enough said. Additionally quite a few other clubs including Glasgow Rangers, Blackpool, Dundee and Plymouth Argyle seemed to have adopted the song, which clearly shows its allure but is also a tad annoying.

Apart from this shining example there is absolutely no goal music that should ever be considered because it is just plain wrong. Take Scotland where it was decided in their infinite wisdom to hold a poll to decide which song they wanted to use at Hampden Park for the rare sight of a Scottish goal being scored. I'm sorry but if you don't know which song to use then that suggests there is no serious candidate and so any competition to find the most suitable tune is immediately and fundamentally flawed. The notion of asking the public has been taken way too far.

Undeterred, the Scottish FA continued with their search and ended up with Bits & Pieces as their choice. No, not another Dave Clark Five classic which would have been vaguely understandable but some Hardbag 1990s rave concoction remixes. It's not exactly the sort of jaunty tune you normally associate with this environment. Mind you when the other choices were the incumbent 500 Miles by The Proclaimers or the god-forsaken Chelsea Dagger by The Fratellis then you can sympathise with the Scottish fans.

As we are on the subject of Chelsea Dagger there is absolutely no excuse for any playing of this so-called song ever inside or outside the confines of a football stadium. So when I learned that of all clubs, that scion of style Juventus use it I was flabbergasted and distraught at the travesty and injustice of it all. Although that sympathy for the Scots does not last too long when you realise that one other option available was no goal music whatsoever. Not since Ally's Tartan Army came back from Argentina in 1978 with their tails tucked firmly between their legs or the unveiling of their pink, white and yellow monstrosity of a kit in 2014, have the Scots suffered such a toe-curling national embarrassment.

The problem is getting so bad that one suspects that teams will start to deliberately avoid scoring just so they can escape the humiliation of hearing the refrain of their chosen goal music. Imagine the post-match interview "Sure, the points are always important but we decided as a team that we could no longer listen to that bilge one more time. We would rather go down than have to suffer hearing that blasted out over the PA. It's important that the fans realise that the whole team was behind this decision and not just one individual."

But if you think we have it bad in the UK just venture into Europe to find some absolute horrors. Quite how Hannover 96 ended up with the asinine Nellie the Elephant nobody knows, or at least nobody is admitting to know. This calumny should be investigated by FIFA, UEFA, Interpol and the FBI combined and no one can sleep easy in their beds until the person responsible is tracked down and dealt with in the most severe manner possible. Paris St Germain blotted their copybook with a rendition of Uptown Funk being blasted out as soon as the net bulged. Imagine thinking Mark Ronson should ever be allowed into a football stadium? Laughable really.

It is not just cod pop songs that are used either there is also the liberal slaying of classical music, which is generally used as the teams enter the pitch as opposed to celebrating a goal but it is still not right. Aside from the god awful Champions League theme tune which is a badly mangled, disfigured version of Handel's 'Bartok the Priest' that quite rightly gets booed by Man City fans, there are the dark, foreboding notes of Wagner's Ride of the Valkyries that has been known to blast out from the odd ground to strike fear into the hearts of the opposition. Am not sure how Wagner's Ring cycle made it into clubs' conscience but it needs to be removed before any further damage is inflicted.

A further development that has transcended the musical faux pas to sully the enjoyment of a goal was announced by Atletico Madrid in conjunction with their main sponsor, Philips, when their move to their new ground the Wanda Metropolitano, will be accompanied by the stadium bursting into flashes of red and white - the club's colours – when a goal is scored. So not only are our ears going to get a bashing but our eyes will be assailed as well. Cue the next idea of scented goal celebrations and remember where you heard it first.

The biggest issue with goal music is that it stunts and strangles any spontaneous goal celebration, which is one of the few pleasures left in football. The release of all that pent-up frustration used to find a handy conduit but not when that chance is stifled by tasteless songs that are foisted upon us. If having to listen to The Piranhas' Tom Hark is not bad enough already then being drowned out by it is totally unacceptable. It is injurious to your health as well as being an infringement of human rights, so please make it stop.

Maybe there is one more possible use of goal music that could warrant consideration. What about an apposite tune for an own goal? We all love a comic own goal and what better way to deepen the embarrassment of the player responsible than having a song highlighting their utter incompetence. Just imagine Britney Spears' magnus opus Oops, I Did it Again playing at full volume in the aftermath of a howler. There could not be a more excellent embellishment of a poignant moment and it has to be a sure fire winner.

GRAPHICS

Of all the many useful developments in football analytics, it is the heat maps, the stupid, facile, pointless heat maps that have made it big. They're even on Match of the Day now and that show used to be the last bastion of resistance to this sort of thing.

Iain Macintosh from The Set Pieces' Pieces of Hate

At their very best graphics illustrate a point or a series of points with one striking image. Encapsulating various bits of data in a visually appealing manner is an art and we bow down to the ingenuity behind them. The importance of data cannot be denied as the raft of data analysts involved in football continues to grow apace and clubs like Southampton have managed to harness the power of using such information to great effect.

But there is a considerable downside to this current phenomenon in that people have got a wee bit carried away and lost sight of their original purpose. In fact there are graphics that go in the opposite direction and rather than clarify they obfuscate, leaving the poor punter confused and disoriented. Then there is the thorny problem of how fans interpret the data to serve their own ends so skilful players are castigated for not covering the same amount of ground as a more technically limited midfield water carrier.

One of the more recent additions to the list of graphics is the wagon wheel of passes. Now considering the average player will total over 40 passes in a match there is not a great deal of insight to be gained. Whilst the top teams such as Bayern Munich and Barcelona can get close to 1,000 passes between them, there is not much to be gained in insight when faced with a diagram that looks as though it was drawn by a spider on a whole heap of hallucinogenic drugs. These diagrams are less about illustration and more about obfuscation satisfying nobody apart from those that create them, so they are really a rather self-serving exercise.

Then take Heat Maps. No really, please do take Heat Maps, as far away as possible as they add nothing to our understanding of the game apart from a splash of garish colours that some odd impressionist painter might churn out. Their proliferation as part of the post-match analysis induces migraines in anyone unfortunate to get too close to the fluorescent mix of reds, greens and oranges that make absolutely no sense. Indeed at first sight it looks like a gorilla has been dipping its fingers in the paint pots and has been allowed to run free, unchecked whilst it runs amok smearing a blank canvas with more colour than is strictly necessary and in a dangerously arbitrary manner.

During the next stage of recognition it dawns on us that this may be a weather map with some pretty serious storms on the way. The sort of thing where the weather anchor warns you to batten down the hatches and stay indoors. But you would be much mistaken, as this is meant to help you understand how your team got so badly battered in their last game. The acid test is that the Heat Map often requires a fair few paragraphs of explanation, which is surely defeating the object somewhat of a picture being worth a thousand words. Beneath the picture there are at least a thousand words if not more.

To add insult to injury these Heat Maps are then turned into 'hilarious' piss-takes when cartoon penises are added to suggest that your team got a real dicking. Oh hold my sides as they are about to split open. Naturally when you have been thrashed within an inch of your lives the thing you really need is some smart arse to rub it in with knobs on, literally and metaphorically. So now these graphics are being used to make you feel even worse than you did originally, which is pretty close to some form of sadistic cruelty.

Another element of graphics, which has troubled me for a while now, is the possession pie chart. As we are all beginning to realise possession is not actually 9/10th of the law anymore and you have to qualify the sort of possession a team enjoys. Endless passing between the back four and the newly-installed sweeper-keeper is not exactly threatening the other team and with that hoary old adage that it only takes a second to score a goal apparently the ball needs to be in the other half unless you are David Beckham or Nayim or Xavi Alonso, well you get my drift.

Also how do they monitor the possession percentages when the ball is out of play? Considering on average the football is 'dead' for at least 15 minutes of every game how is that reflected in the charts? If a side is due to take a throw-in or a free-kick how does that get shown and should we not have another chart showing this as an adjunct to the main one? So we could have two charts one for 'live' and one for 'dead' possession, now that would be something to behold and really enlighten us.

Some poor, deluded souls actually go as far as getting such things made into t-shirts and walk around in public with them emblazoned on their chest. These are the same people who wear Ramones t-shirts with the sadly mistaken belief that the only song they released is Baby, I Love You. So rather than allowing the graphic mafia or 'graphia' to run riot can we please start restricting their use and go back to the days when we could watch a game without being assailed by this lurid representation of the stats?

Imagine the horror that the majestic, imperious doyen of football writing Hugh McIlvanney would feel if one of his majestic pieces was daubed with these garish graphics and multi-coloured monstrosities. There would be an almighty stramash and a flurry of Caledonian invective from the Scot that would turn the air blue rather than a combination of pink, puce and psychedelic purple.

 ## HALF-AND-HALF SCARVES & SHIRTS

We started doing them [half–and–half scarves] for international rugby, and it spread into English football. Our competitors picked up on it.

Claire Dolan, partner in Arena Scarves in an interview with the BBC.

If anybody needs any evidence of how wrong half-and-half scarves are, the fact that they originated out of rugby union means they need to look no further. We have all seen them and I am hoping we have all done the right thing and either ignored them completely or destroyed the offending articles on the grounds of good taste.

There are plenty of things that can annoy me during a game but not many things that can actually put me into a bad mood before the match has even started, but this particular abomination manages to do so in spades. Nobody needs this thrust into their face on their approach to the ground. Surely the police should step in and do their duty by taking them away for mass incineration. There is also the product extension that besmirches anyone involved with this ghastly trade the half-and-half shirt that takes everything to a new level of crassness.

The half-and-half scarf started as a way of commemorating a particularly noteworthy European match or the odd Cup Final. There were even the occasional so-called 'friendship scarves' as clubs struck allegiances with clubs from other countries such as Chelsea and Glasgow Rangers. Weird but true. Surely a match programme is a far better method of remembering a particular match rather than a tawdry piece of old tat? That this has now become a regular sight outside most grounds is an unseemly blight on the landscape of British football, with every fixture now being deemed worthy of such a scarf. Even the most unattractive, meaningless fixture is considered to merit such memorabilia. Forgive me if you have a Stoke / Hull scarf hanging proudly in your sitting room above the mantelpiece but that is absolutely nonsensical in every way, shape and form.

The sellers even try to dress these up as so-called 'souvenir scarves' but there is a fundamental flaw behind this premise considering a souvenir is defined as a memento of an occasion. If the game is against a team that you are not overly bothered about you will not need or want a souvenir because it means very little. If however, it is against one of your main rivals then the idea of wearing their colours is one that rubs against the very essence of football support. So either way the last thing on the earth you will be yearning after is one of these shameful pieces of paraphernalia. Then of course they have the date of the match proudly displayed, which gives it some sort of 'exclusive' tag in the evil minds of the creators.

I have never actually witnessed anyone buying a half-and-half scarf but one must assume that they do get sold in fair quantities otherwise the sellers would not be there every single match. They must have some barefaced cheek these guys as they do not seem to mind the unveiled scorn that nearly every right-minded fan shows them as they peddle their wares shamelessly. In fact so appalling is the merchandise that it would be more appropriate if they were selling them far away from the public's gaze, down dark alleyways out of dodgy basements.

Perhaps the most noxious element of this whole farrago is the attempted post-match sale, as you troop off into the darkening streets, humbled by another home defeat they are still trying to flog you the bloody things. As if I wanted to be reminded of the most recent humiliation. There is only place that this scarf should be used and that is not for tying around your own neck but rather around the bloke trying to flog you one and then suspending him from the nearest lamppost.

In trying to imagine the potential customers there are a variety of images that arise, nearly all of them highly disturbing. Most of them appropriately enough would be half-wits. In the end there are probably just a few hundred quite strange individuals who have been busy collecting them and have their spare room dedicated to them alongside their pet cockroaches and their assortment of Slipknot albums. Like some sort of strange sect their life's mission is to gather as many half-and-half scarves and then meet up to compare them all under candlelight in a forest just outside Droitwich.

According to the few freaks who defend half-and-half scarves their justification is that these appalling pieces of knitwear are principally aimed at the football tourist, whoever they might be. So for all those individuals who have just popped over from Shanghai to take in some of the Premier League action, this is the sorry result. With no particular affinity to either club they can shamelessly enjoy the balance provided by these wretched items. Well in the true tradition of uncompromising honesty they can go do one and never darken our doors again. Football is centred on passion and rivalry, not equanimity and even-handedness. We need bias, the more blatant the better, otherwise the game descends into a miasma of the middle ground, as represented by the half-and-half scarf.

Full credit must be given to the Trafford pub in Manchester that has banned any customers from wearing any of these abominations on their premises. So if you did happen to have one wrapped around your sorry neck you were advised to throw them into the nearby bin in order to clear your conscience. Now that is the sort of local action that we would expect and hope to see extended throughout the land.

The very fact that they are also known as Friendship scarves pretty much sums up their worth and relevance. Football is not about friendship it is about impassioned rivalry spiced up with a touch of vitriol and most certainly not about amiability or getting on with the opposition's fans. If we were seeking friendship we would sit at home and join a dating site or something similar. We go to football to rant, rave and even rile the opposition. Anything else is watering down the rawness of the experience and is certainly not what we are in search of when we go to the match.

We will leave the last word with Claire Dolan who is quoted at the very beginning of this chapter. "Fans should get into the 21st Century. The old days of it being quite so tribal...we need to get away from that." Well actually Claire we are more than happy to stay well away from your vision of what football is like. We enjoy the enmity and the squabbling. Tribal we are and tribal we will remain, thanks very much.

**It is not panic or fear or revenge. It was exhilaration...
I am attracted to the moment when consciousness ceases:
the moment of survival, of animal intensity, of violence...
I felt that I had literally become weightless...
that crowd violence was their drug.**

Excerpt from "Among the Thugs" by Bill Buford

There was a period, a far from glorious one, in English football history when the focus of the media was less on events on the pitch and much more on what was going on the terraces. Stadiums became the playground of the violent. The lurid headlines portrayed hooligans roaming the land with exotic tribal names, such as the Zulus and Headhunters, terrorising local communities with reckless abandon. The 1970s and 1980s in particular were plagued by regular outbreaks of violence, in fact the regularity became such that it was unusual for a weekend to pass without some trouble 'kicking off'.

This sort of civil disorder did not go down well with Margaret Thatcher and set football on a collision course with the authorities. Out of these unhappy and dark times a few years later after the dust had settled, a new genre of books was spawned. The hooligan diary became a fixture on the bookshelves and they were churned out with monotonous frequency, as each tried to outdo each other with more lurid tales of their adventures travelling up and down the country causing mayhem in their respective firms. It all becomes rather repetitive and tiresome but the writers do not seem remotely bothered about that and plough on regardless. Obviously they feel that you cannot get enough fisticuffs.

I am not sure how many times we need to read about how the ICF 'proper mullered' the Geordies or how the Baby Squad 'sorted out' the Naughty Forty. Of course nearly every single book comes with the plea that this is not about glorifying violence but is trying to find the causes behind the trouble and shed new light on the reasons. Only for each one to proceed to glorify violence at every opportunity. We learn very little from the vast majority of these poorly written, under-researched confessionals apart from the fact Billy was as hard as nails whilst Scotty was all mouth and no trousers. It really is lowest common denominator stuff and they become increasingly difficult to read as the lack of substance and variety in the many tales produces an indigestible diet of undiluted thuggery. In the end the reader is as battered and bruised as the poor sods who lose out in the countless battles within the books to the point of being punch drunk.

The natural consequence of the plethora of books was the next stage in glorification. Bill Buford's 1990 book Among the Thugs, quoted in the introduction to this chapter, is one of the better books in portraying this and the fact that it was written by an American tells us a great deal about the quality of the others. Out of this sudden rush to go to print, films were soon following in their wake. One of the first of its kind was The Football Factory back in 2004, which had the usual cocktail of violence, sex, drugs, alcohol and a smattering of football mixed in just for fun. The Football Factory's central character, played of course by the soft man's hard man Danny Dyer, is driven by the unholy trinity of "thieving, fucking and fighting." We do not move too far beyond these pillars of wisdom in most of the films that poured forth in satiating the thirst for violence. And Dyer's so-called acting managed to make Vinnie Jones look like a cross between Robert de Niro and Sir Laurence Olivier.

If anyone has had the misfortune to see Green Street you have my every sympathy. The BBC review sums up the critical panning it received – "Green Street would be a grittily convincing study of football violence, were it not for two factors. The first is Elijah Woods, a pint-sized, baby-faced actor who makes the least plausible hooligan in cinema history. The second is co-star Charlie Hunnam, who is the leader of the West Ham firm and sports the worst Cock-er-nee accent since Dick Van Dyke's in Mary Poppins."

Then, almost inevitably, there is "Green Street II" which as sequels go is almost an insult to the original, some achievement in truth. It is also something of an anomaly that many of these films featured American actors as this adds to the lack of authenticity. One wonders why the filmmakers decided that it would be such a good idea to import this talent. It almost makes you yearn for an appearance by Danny Dyer for some authenticity.

Whilst much of the so-called action in these films is based on fact there were undoubtedly embellishments and the whole unedifying idea of glorifying violence made its mark. There is a worrying sense of reverence, almost verging on idolisation of the hardest nutcases involved in this grubby, grimy underworld. It seems strange now looking back at such a portrayal as the football experience has been mainly sanitised and whilst nobody would suggest the problems have gone away, they are nowhere near being on the same scale as they were thirty years ago. Nobody in their right mind would attempt to recreate them, but recreate them they do. It is neither big nor clever and just remember the net result of all this is that Danny Dyer now has a career. I will just leave it there.

We are extremely disappointed that Luis Suarez did not shake hands with Patrice Evra before yesterday's game... He has not only let himself down but also Kenny Dalglish, his team-mates and the club. It has been made absolutely clear to Luis Suarez that his behaviour was not acceptable.

Ian Ayre, Liverpool managing director.

The furore that followed a non-handshake in 2012 suggests the importance of the pre-match handshake has grown out of all proportion to its genuine worth. The condemnation from Suarez's own club was almost as severe as when he took a sizeable chunk out of Branislav Ivanovic's shoulder. It was a pretty stupid and childish thing to do but it was hardly on the same scale as many of the other misdemeanours on the Uruguayan's lengthy and colourful charge sheet. All sense of perspective seems to have been lost in this profusion of chumminess and false bonhomie that now accompanies any match.

The whole farrago of the pre-match handshaking festival is all part of the show. Whereas before it was just that slightly awkward shake between the captains, now you have the long line before every game which was all meant to illustrate the enormous amount of respect that fellow professionals have for each other. A conservative estimate puts the number of handshakes at a shade under 200 including each player shaking opposing players' hand as well as the match officials. This practice began in 2004 but this is not the only sort of handshake that is giving football a bad reputation.

Possibly on the surface handshakes are the most innocent of human interaction, a semi-formal way of acknowledging a fellow human being but look beneath and you may well find there is a lot more than meets the eye. Considering those ever so secretive and rather sinister Freemasons indulge in particular types of handshake there should be some sort of alert to the unwary of the potential dangers that lie therein. There is clearly something far more worrying behind this and it has started to become a real problem right in the midst of football, it is the Trojan Horse that nobody has noticed.

There was a time when a handshake was as animated as players got as they celebrated a goal, they might even stretch to a ruffle of the hair or a pat on the back if it was a truly exceptional effort but that was it. And of course there is now the pre-match rigmarole of all the players lining up to shake their opponents hands, which in itself is pretty meaningless and just forms part of the set routine. It is all a little bland and beige and the only time anyone takes notice is when a player for whatever reason ducks the handshake and sets tongues wagging.

When Luis Suarez opted to ignore Patrice Evra's outstretched hand in 2012 there was an uproar that still rumbles on today and gets mentioned in the same breath as his various biting indiscretions. That such a fuss should be made about missing a handshake is not unusual. Wayne Bridge did a similar swerve on John Terry because of the Chelsea captain's alleged dalliance with Bridge's wife and he undoubtedly had the vast majority of the watching public on his side. So there are times when handshakes should be avoided at all costs but these lessons do not seemed to have been learned by everybody. Some poor, misguided fools continue to openly indulge in doing it without fear of being reprimanded.

There is also the farce that is the managers' handshakes that drip with insincerity. The times when Arsene Wenger has to shake Jose Mourinho's hand prior to the game is one of those moments when you know that both would rather have their hands gripped firmly around the other's throat. Then we have the entertainment of the post-match shake, which so often gets lost somehow as the vanquished tries to avoid the victor at all costs for that ever so awkward shake, hurrying down the tunnel to avoid any chance of direct contact. If this is not possible the cursory nature of the handshake is such that it can be easy to miss it through blinking.

There is one other variety of handshake that would be more accurately described as a hand slap and this is administered when a player has been substituted. Whilst the substituted player is usually greeted enthusiastically, unsurprisingly by the player replacing him, he may also get a consoling pat on the arm from the manager for his troubles. More often than not it is the most cursory of nods in recognition that the player has failed hence why he is being removed from the action. Feeling a little sorry for himself the player seeks the solace of the bench where his colleagues are cooped up like so many battery chickens awaiting their fate.

This is where the fun begins as the player goes down the long line exchanging warm hand slaps in return. With each successive slap there is slightly less enthusiasm than the previous one and in the end there is barely any contact whatsoever. This ritual even takes place if the player in question has given away a penalty after earlier shanking the ball into his own net to give the opposition an unassailable lead. As hollow gestures go this is right up there with FIFA's Respect campaign. In truth if they did let their true feelings be aired they would be snubbing the subbed and using another hand gesture which is slightly more vigorous but less pleasant.

Perhaps the most irritating of all though also includes a player about to be substituted, as he wends his sorry way off the pitch and probably a little wary of the warmth of his reception by his manager and team-mates, he decides to hone in on the only man who cannot deny him the pleasure of a reciprocal shake. The unsuspecting individual is minding his own business and carrying out his admin when the player is right in his face and offering his hand in a 'I shall not be denied' manner. The poor old referee is caught and cannot escape so limply he will accept the outstretched hand as he tries to hide his disdain for such over-familiarity.

It is abundantly clear that the last thing the referee would want to do is to shake hands, but there is an element of force majeure involved in the awkward exchange. It would be cruel and a little complex to do what he really feels like doing which is to show a red card for such cringe worthy sycophancy. It may not be in the FA Rules handbook but this sort of behaviour needs to be stamped out before we reach the point of an endless procession of handshakes punctuating every game and turning them into festivals of faux friendliness.

One of the principal reasons we go to football is to see a contest and ideally a fierce contest at that. We want a gladiatorial spirit where no quarter is given and the teams are it tooth and claw from the very off. We certainly do not come to see an outbreak of brotherliness that stretches across the whole canvas from prior to kick-off through to the less than bitter end. If this continues at the current rate there will be the prospect of fans going for a round of handshakes with their rivals after the match and then all off home for a nice cup of tea.

Then just when we thought that things could not get any worse up pops the evolution of the ludicrously contrived celebratory handshake as practiced by Harry Kane and Dele Alli amongst others. This tricksy piece of nonsense is so convoluted and complex that it beggars belief and actually detracts from any praise that the goal that spawned the idea might have merited. In fact I would go as far as to say that this should be bracketed with the dab as a punishable crime. Yes it is that horrendous.

The amount of time these two England internationals must have spent perfecting their routine would probably exceed the number of hours that England traditionally last in major tournaments. These are the sort of hand movements that would be the preserve of particularly irritating and self-obsessed teenagers. As someone rightly pointed out at the time they warrant a retrospective ban of some length, although the worry is that they would use that time to rehearse another contrived fluttering of hands and fist bumps. In fact if any of the boys from the under-12s or Under-13s that I coach were to attempt something similar they would be substituted immediately.

You have to go back to the very first season of the Premier League for a worrying precedence there was the infamous Ryan Giggs Paul Ince ensemble. And so we had the unsightly and unsettling vision of watching two internationals of some repute bending down to meet each other, touching hands and then retreating in a comic Chaplinesque style. Oh how we chuckled back then in the early 1990s. Giggs may be lauded as one of the greatest players of the last twenty years mainly for his incredible longevity but this does cast a shadow over his legacy. He should have known better than displaying this sort of tomfoolery.

HIPSTERS

A fake football fan. More likely to be seen on the internet than in the stadium, where he usually annoys the real football fans with his smugness, while knowing shit about the game. Follows trendy teams like Dortmund and Napoli and is the first to leave the sinking ship.

Definition from The Urban Dictionary

The main problem with becoming the most popular game in the world is that there is always the odd element of the audience that are not particularly desirable. There are the hangers-on who ruin the party. Along with the wheat comes the chaff and amongst the many millions of people devoted to the game there is usually one group that should, with the best will in the world, be run out of town and made to live the rest of their lives in splendid isolation on a remote island in the Outer Hebrides. The good news is that this particular crew are immediately recognisable and will never be able to hide so rounding them up should be no issue.

Hipsters have suddenly got football and it is terrifying. Having shunned the game for a while they are suddenly all over it like a rash, or a tight knit Juventus back four. You can spot them from a mile off. The first aspect of their appearance that will strike you is the forest of hair that smothers the lower part of their faces. Yes, ladies and gentlemen, the beard is back and the luxuriant growth these guys have developed is an all-encompassing feature that knows no limits. It is pretty much de rigeur for them to have more hair beneath the lip than above their eyebrows and it is not unknown for said beards to have baubles hanging off them in a rather louche manner.

It is somewhat surprising that such profuse facial hair is the choice of a group who are never far away from a frothy cappuccino as the unhealthy result is an almost continuous dribbling of said product into the beard, making it all rather straggly and quite frankly unkempt. This occupational hazard is proof of how the hipster likes to live their life on the edge alongside their ultra approach to football support. Not content with arriving at matches on their scooters the hipsters make the match day experience as complete as possible with a vast range of activities that separate them from mere mortals.

There is the choice of glasses which is so crucial and has far-reaching consequences that none of us can truly fathom. The Klopp-style spectacles are now ever so slightly last season, and things do move very rapidly in the world of hipster fandom. It has been rumoured that the next big thing is going to be the achingly trendy monocle that will be the talk of the terraces sooner than you might imagine.

But let's get back to basics. First of all, the choice of match is of paramount importance. No Premier League big time Charlies for our intrepid crew, in fact anything above tier 6 in the football pyramid is a little too close to the bone. So they delve deeply into the joys of The Isthmian Ryman Premier League where the likes of Dulwich Hamlet are to be found strutting their stuff. In fact Dulwich Hamlet are pretty much the epitome of a hipster's favourite club. From their slightly unusual kit of mauve and pink, which looks so good in the Angoran wool knitted scarf and bobble hat combo that draws so many covetous glances from the fashionistas, to the rather unusual name – surely the only football club to have incorporated a Shakespeare play.

Dulwich ticks the boxes as it is also one of a host of clubs that have genuine fan representation and that is an absolute must for the hipster. He would not find himself dead following a team with a shady owner, thus ruling out the vast majority of League clubs in an instant. His voice needs to be heard at the AGM and beyond so it must be part of the DNA of any club hoping to attract the invaluable support of our bearded friends.

During the match itself the hipster's behaviour is a combination of maintaining a necessary aloofness from the events on the pitch and a complete mastery of the various tactics being employed. It's all part of the bigger picture, the key is to not get dragged into the minutiae such as the score on the day but more to understanding how this game fits in to the holistic approach to the universe of football. Being able to carry off such insouciance with a keen eye for detail is not something that you can just do, it takes years of careful study and training. Welcome to the Hipster Academy.

Hipsters also have a way of acknowledging fellow hipsters with a warm, almost intimate hug but no more and no less. Touching beards is definitely off limits so one must approach this form of greeting with care. It is notoriously easy to get this one wrong and as much practising as is feasible is encouraged, especially after a couple of cheeky craft beers produced in the local micro brewery, which used to be a public convenience, hence the catchy name of its most popular beverage - Piss Pour. The fact that this particular ale has a hint of coriander and a cheeky dash of chilli that make this concoction all the more acceptable but thoroughly undrinkable, represents a minor inconvenience to the hipster.

Of course the hipster is not confined to these shores and is often seen catching a flight to Europe early on a Sunday morning so as not to miss out on a well-earned trip to a crucial fixture in the Austrian Erste Liga, or Second Division to you and me. Wacker Innsbruck taking on SV Horn at the charming Tivoli-Neu stadium is a fixture that really gets the blood flowing with the best hot chocolate this side of the Alps as the perfect accompaniment. Who would have thought that those lederhosen would look so good in the Dulwich Hamlet colours? And as for those specks of chocolate splattered over the beard, they are simply to die for.

There are a couple of do-nots that hipsters need to avoid at all costs. Never wear a replica football shirt unless it is one of the Chosen Five – Borussia Dortmund, Real Oviedo, River Plate, Sassuolo or St. Pauli. Those shirts should never be the standard issue and most certainly not man made fibres, only cotton, wool or silk are allowed. Under no circumstances, dare to criticise a goalless draw, which as we all know is the purest expression of football as an art form. Refrain from getting involved with twitter unless it is in a mildly ironic tone and do not follow any official accounts.

It is strictly forbidden to start quoting Albert Camus, Vladimir Nabokov or indeed any other literary figure who happens to have mentioned football in their writing; this is the stuff of philistines and to be studiously swerved to save the humiliation of being lumped together with the general mass of football fans who are desperately trying to better themselves. Hipsters have a self-assurance and a swagger that that sets them apart and all these rules must be adhered to otherwise the crucial gap between the hipster and the ordinary fan might be getting a little too close for comfort.

The hipster will continue in his own sweet way to navigate the choppy waters of football support with his own blend of aloofness and arrogance, so it is best not to stand in his way as he glides serenely onwards and upwards. It is certainly a charmed life they lead and however ridiculous they may seem to any outsiders their unshakeable belief that they are in the right remains as resolute and healthy as their well-groomed beards.

INTERNATIONAL FRIENDLIES / BREAK

How have FIFA been allowed to gradually sneak in these huge interruptions to a season, which the overwhelming majority of fans who put club before country despise? They've become so frequent they can no longer be described as a break, but the resumption of international fixtures.

Brian Reade, Daily Mirror October 2016

It is rather difficult to ascertain exactly what these matches are meant to achieve apart from picking up unnecessary injuries, showing how countless substitutions can ruin the pattern of a match, and generally annoying and alienating all club managers as they lose their players to niggles and knocks. They are also quite often a misnomer as the friendly turns into a petulant contest further increasing the chance of someone being stricken with a serious injury. Michel Platini, former head of UEFA, decided he had had enough of this charade announcing plans to turn these into a qualification process for the European Championships, which seems a little daft but does point to the futility of international friendlies.

Although there is still the deeply concerning issue that when these friendlies take place at Wembley there are usually in the region of 80,000 people who actually volunteer to watch 'the action' unfold and indeed pay for the privilege. One has to wonder what these people would be doing if they weren't dutifully turning up to watch this charade of a match, maybe they would be playing charades at home with Auntie Nellie and this is their only chance of escape?

One redeeming feature for England is that these matches are at least mildly competitive whereas most of their qualifying matches are against teams that would struggle in League Two. To add fuel to the fire when these friendlies are responsible for the dreaded international break then we have reached the gates of Armageddon with supporters struggling to cope with the sheer pointlessness of it all. If Samuel Beckett were still alive I am sure he would have written something about it along the lines of Waiting for the International Break.

With the majority of fans siding with club over country, these international breaks are major irritants and nearly always come at the wrong time. Your team has just started to gain some momentum from a handful of unbeaten games when along comes an enforced fortnight off and they return to square one immediately, reverting to a long series of dismal performances. Or the team reaches new depths of awfulness just prior to the break and there is now a full two weeks outpouring of grief to bemoan the lack of quality in the squad and face up to the inevitability of relegation. Whichever way, the international break is a massive pain in the arse and generally loathed by all and sundry for interrupting the flow of the domestic season at precisely the wrong time.

One of the other downsides of the international break is the huge vacuum that is created. Just take a look at Gillette Soccer Saturday when they send the reserves in. We all know that Jeff Stelling is irreplaceable so when his deputy Julian Warren appears there is always a sense of anti-climax. It is not that Warren is that bad, he does an acceptable job but it is just not Stelling. The attempts at witty repartee with the panel are just a little too forced and unnatural to work. Added to which the panel is filled with those who would normally be stuck in a gusty gantry at Boundary Park or squeezed up against a wall inside the WHAM stadium. It is when Iain Dowie or Matt Murray become centre stage that the problems start to mount up. You know you have reached the point of no return when you start pining for a bon mot from Charlie Nicholas or the rapier-like wit of Paul Merson.

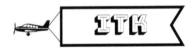

The only true wisdom is in knowing you know nothing.

Socrates, the classical Greek philosopher,
rather than the classical Brazilian footballer.

ITK is not a second division Greek outfit, nor a new video game, nor even a sexually transmitted disease just in case you were wondering. ITK stands for In The Know and incorporates a whole breed of spotty little twerps who spend their daylight hours locked in their bedrooms, hunched over their computers whilst concocting the latest guff to fill the acres of space that exist in the world of social media. Also known as keyboard warriors they keep themselves busy by claiming to have the low-down on the very latest transfer moves wherever and whenever they may be happening.

Their 'knowledge' is limitless as they can make this shit up all day long without truth ever complicating matters. As a natural consequence of their nocturnal lifestyle you never actually get to meet them face-to-face, which is a crying shame as there are a few things you would like to do with their faces if you got the chance. From behind the enveloping cloak of anonymity they launch themselves on the unsuspecting public who are often duped into believing what they say.

The way it works is these IDK-ers start a rumour about a player being on the move and from that very slight premise the whole domino effect is triggered whereby a raft of players are then going hither and thither with reckless abandon. When challenged as to the veracity of these snippets of information they point to the evidence of that central midfielder who moved from CSKA Moscow to Sporting Lisbon back in 2013 as they had predicted three months before. I suppose one out of 578 ain't bad but it is not something on which to base a career, I would humbly suggest.

The issue here is that they are so relentless in the creation of rumours that by sheer weight of numbers they are bound to get one right now and again. They are not short of chutzpah and will crow endlessly about their unerring accuracy whilst blithely ignoring that a success rate of 0.0017 is not something that people are usually proud of but whatever, keep fighting the good fight. It may be a numbers game but these folk are very selective about which numbers count so undeterred by facts on they plough with letting us know just how they are so well connected, having the inside track on almost every league, team or player you care to mention and a fair few you do not.

There is also a worrying correlation between these rumours and certain betting odds that makes one slightly wary of their motives. Basically treat with extreme caution anything they spew out. In the old days they used to be called spivs but they did not have the advantage of technology to spread the word. Their so-called sources include a raft of shady agents and anonymous intermediaries. Imagine claiming such characters as the provenance for all your invaluable facts.

As mentioned these grubby urchins are generally nocturnal animals, rarely seen in daylight and this is especially true of their two main hibernation periods in September and January in the time that leads up to their moment of truth known as Transfer Deadline Day. This is basically their Christmas Day and the lucky beggars have two of them, which stretch over the space of a couple of months. This is the time when everyone is on the hunt for the slightest snippet and boy do they make sure we have snippets aplenty when these guys are unleashed.

One of the other key features of this group and their sources, which are variously described as agents, intermediaries or even if they are being particularly bold, insiders, is that they can never be challenged. Being the fount of all knowledge must be particularly demanding and it is very good of them to share this with the nation rather than keeping it to themselves rework this, the challenged/challenge repetition is a bit awkward. However sorely they must be tempted to keep all the goodies locked away their altruism knows no bounds and they divulge this information to the great unwashed.

There is a faint suspicion that a lot of these so-called insiders are not as well-informed as many would like us to think and that they are in the process of flying a kite. This impression is reinforced when images of cloak and dagger characters are used in their respective avatars. The fine principle of never trusting a man in a hat has never been more valid. Nobody begrudges the odd speculative punt but please do not insult our intelligence in claiming that this is anything more than that.

They really do outreach themselves this particular breed when it comes to fixture release day. So confident are they of their own omniscience that they claim to have prior knowledge of the fixtures and can therefore reveal your club's schedule for the coming season before any official announcement from the respective league. But before you start checking your diary and provisionally booking your travel arrangements, it may be worth waiting for confirmation because now and again these predictions do not quite go according to plan. To avoid ending up in Middlesbrough or Barnsley on a Tuesday November night with no match to go to and nothing to do, it may be best to not rely on the veracity of these endless chancers for any information insider or otherwise.

But before you can chastise these unreliable sources and goad them for their wild inaccuracies they disappear off the face of the earth. No doubt they are busy returning to burying themselves underneath the stone from which they first crawled and spending a few days reinventing themselves with a new avatar and a fresh raft of absolute nonsense with which to blind us once more. It is neither big nor clever but there are hordes of them still out there, roaming the land without checks or balances, so beware and do not fall into the trap of the ITK and their group of oily acolytes.

It is telling to realise that the man widely regarded as one of the very first ITKers, a certain Duncan Jenkins was the figment of someone's imagination and was created to wind up those that slavishly followed every word, every whisper. As Mike Henson described him in an article for The Set Pieces "Jenkins was a 'perspiring' football writer who couldn't write. A wannabee without an ounce of self-awareness, but a surplus of self-belief." The Jenkins persona was the creation of Sean Cummins, a Liverpool fan who lived in Manchester. For three years between 2009 and his untimely death in 2012 Jenkins was the inside man at Anfield who revealed the line-ups on match day before anyone else or who gave the scoop on transfers.

Jenkins' fame / infamy reached such a point that Cummins was met by Liverpool's new director of communications, Jen Chang who told him to stop or there would be sanctions taken against him by the club including revoking his season ticket. Chang strenuously denied the meeting when it came out but he left the club a few months later as fact started to challenge fiction for the most dramatic denouement and Cummins' double life was over. No more Mister ITK.

JOKER IN THE PACK

He's very talented but he's also as daft as a brush.

Bobby Robson on Paul Gascoigne

There's always one in every squad. The rascal intent on being the clown prince, hell-bent on causing chaos and anarchy and making a bloody nuisance of himself. He's unstoppable this man, with an endless supply of hilarious practical jokes to play on his unsuspecting colleagues. Although it is not such a surprise, neither is it that funny, in fact they are right royal pains in the arse with their forced bonhomie and weak wisecracks. They are under the illusion that they are essential for team spirit but their infantile behaviour is a sad indictment of these desperate, pathetic attention seekers. They are masters of self-justification and self-delusion.

It is mainly Paul Gascoigne's fault as he was always portrayed as the ultimate jester and he just happened to be a simply wonderful footballer and then players must have thought that his magic would rub off on them if they played the giddy goat. Ultimately they all failed as they hardly had a fraction of the natural talent of Gascoigne. But the japes and the practical jokes just keep rolling on. Unfortunately there is nothing quite as tiresome as forced humour and it very quickly becomes really unfunny.

Gascoigne's infamous belch to a television reporter in Rome in 1993 during his Lazio days did not go down so well with the Italian public. During his brief stay with Middlesbrough he commandeered the team and caused several thousands of pounds worth of damage when almost inevitably he crashed the vehicle. Then there was the moment he did not exactly endear himself to the Norwegians when asked for a few words before a World Cup qualifier in 1992, his quip was blunt and embarrassing - "Yeah, fuck off Norway!"

But despite these and other lapses of judgement the English public adored him and wherever he played, be it Glasgow or Newcastle, London or Liverpool, Rome or Middlesbrough, he was revered because of his incredible talent. Naturally people egged him on to do even worse jokes and japes that were condoned because of the rich, rare artistry he enchanted us with when on the pitch. A lot of his escapades were tasteless and unfunny but this was Gazza so all was forgiven. The idea of the maverick was now firmly established and it was not for the good of our collective health. As a result, training sessions became punctuated by all sorts of tomfoolery and it was de rigeur for every club to have their very own jester.

Mario Balotelli has inherited the mantle with some of his madcap antics whether it be the hilarious setting off of fireworks in his own kitchen, the mock sword fight in an Indian restaurant in Manchester, or the throwing of darts at youth players Balo has done it all and more. In fact he has become the favoured subject of many journalists as he can spawn endless listicles (see List chapter) with his crazy escapades. As with Gascoigne, such outrageous actions are matched with outrageous talent and there is a certain amount of leeway allowed.

But for all the Gascoignes and Balotellis, there are hundreds of players who do not approach their calibre but still insist on trying to emulate them with their puerile pranks. Here is John Beresford on the goings on at St. James's Park "Me and Rob Lee once let Alan Shearer's tyres down," Beresford told talkSPORT. "So he covered my car in crap and, though he denies it, I'm sure he put horse dung down the grill so that when I turned the heating on it reeked." Oh please John don't go on, but he went even further. "I once covered

Lee Clark's BMW in flour. But instead of driving away and letting it all blow off, he decided to wash. All the flour turned to dough and it was ruined." Imagine flour, BMW and Lee Clark all in one fell swoop.

Then we have the series of Rio Ferdinand 'merks' that he inflicted on Ashley Cole, Peter Crouch and most hilariously (sic) Gary Neville. Rio, giggling uncontrollably in the production room, watched a rattled Neville being confronted by bogus police officers about a range of driving offences. The one joke is stretched out to a painful and rather tedious seven minutes or so. But let's move on swiftly and get involved in more merry merks because that's what keeps the world going round.

Be very careful not to find yourself near a football club come April 1st because that is when the demons are truly unleashed and things move into overdrive. Back in 2003 Glasgow Rangers managed to hoodwink the vast majority of their fans when announcing they had signed a Greek striker Yardis Alpolfo for £5 million. The unwary would have missed the fact that his name was an anagram of April Fool's Day. The joke would backfire a few years later when the club went into administration and suffered from a transfer embargo in 2012 before re-emerging as Newco and starting life down in League Two. Maybe they should have squared the circle by announcing the expected transfer of Croatian defender Stan Dinamitroi when they eventually came out of administration the following April. What's that you say, financial meltdown is no joke? Sorry but very little is off limits as far as football comedy is concerned.

As many great philosophers and writers, including Shakespeare, have pointed out madness is close to genius. We should maybe not criticise footballers for falling into the trap. But cutting holes into your room mates' socks, smearing toothpaste on their pillows or stealing their mobiles are not going to win a clutch of comedy awards or make the headlines as they have all been done many times before. If only there was some originality about them it would help but they keep returning to the tried and tested favourites and oh how they laughed until they nearly wet themselves.

But seriously, there is a time and a place for such behaviour and that is in a nursery or kindergarten, not with grown adults playing professional sport. This is not what tactical periodisation is meant to be about and I am pretty sure Messrs Klopp and Guardiola would not see the funny side of such antics. That is the problem with these foreign managers coming over here with no sense of humour and all their gegenpressing confusing us Brits who are just looking for laughs.

K IS FOR KILMARNOCK

A truly crap town, where heroin addicts and stabbings, as well as football violence and pound shops are aplenty.

From Crap Towns Returns book on Kilmarnock

Most English fans have a sneaking affinity with a Scottish team through some loose family connection although please do not tell Kevin Day (see Every Other Team chapter). Mine is with Dundee where my wife was born (Broughty Ferry to be exact) and who also happily have developed a link with my own club Palace, which is almost entirely based on the Manos de Dios who is Julian Speroni. Then there are those who have a Scottish team because of the name, a relationship that would have started by listening to the football results. It may even be down to having a fondness for the colours. But I also have a Scottish team that I cannot stand.

So I must apologise to all those connected with Kilmarnock before they start reading about their club in less than flattering tones . Am not sure if Oscar Wilde ever visited the second largest town in Ayrshire but regardless his words provide some much-needed balm – "There is only one thing in life worse than being talked about and that is not being talked about."

It is utterly irrational but there is something about Kilmarnock that riles me. Situated in those vast nether regions around Glasgow or East Ayrshire to be more specific. There is nothing that distinguishes it from a whole host of similar dormitory towns dotted across the West of Scotland. It does not sound like a great place to visit but I have to admit I have never been there nor have I watched the club, but I just have a deep and enduring antipathy towards Killie. It is rather reassuring to have a Scottish club to hate as it makes the results all the more interesting, adding a bit of spice where previously there was mainly apathy.

Also Killie is a strange sort of a nickname. It is actually a piss poor nickname, being just a lazy abbreviation for those who cannot be bothered with the hassle of too many syllables. 'Come on, Killie' is not exactly a rallying cry to stiffen the sinews and make the opposition quake in their boots. Braveheart it certainly is not. Sounds more like the name for a Shetland pony than a fearsome football outfit. Their main claim to fame is that they are the oldest professional club in Scotland, which is not to be sniffed at as they have nearly reached 150 years in existence. The fact is they have had a century and a half to come up with a decent nickname and settled on Kille. Surely tells us a lot about their ambition and pedigree.

Maybe it is down to the fact that they play at Rugby Park and to put it mildly I am not a big fan of rugby as a game. Apparently they started off as more of a rugby club before morphing into a football club so that could be the stumbling block. Am not sure it is anything to do with the idea of calling your ground something that is connected with another sport. Look at Derby County, who realised the error of their ways when ditching The Baseball Ground for what did become Pride Park for a while before it was then turned into the anodyne iPro stadium. It now seems to have returned to being called Pride Park again. On reflection, I prefer The Baseball Ground, so it is probably not that.

I am sure they are a charming set of people and the fact that they are one of a select bunch of British clubs whose name begins and ends in the same letter clearly gains enormous brownie points with my particular brand of OCD. Furthermore the fact they are one of the few of that select bunch who do not need a suffix like United or Town to qualify makes them even more estimable and on a par with single word clubs such as Liverpool and Celtic. Or maybe it is because they sum up the morass of Scottish clubs that are marooned in the swamp of the Scottish Premier League who make up the numbers, bumping along in the middle, posing no threat to the current Celtic monopoly or the previous Glasgow duopoly. Whatever it is, such antipathy is stronger than any affection for any club north of the border.

Maybe it is their kit that rankles – a fairly dull blue and white striped shirt with blue shorts is not something that stands out from the crowd. It has not changed for a while now and it does not grab the attention or make a statement, it is just rather plain and anonymous, so quite apt for the team that are the object of my ire.

Their current away kit is a great deal more adventurous and does not look too dissimilar to the 1970s classic Peru kit with its diagonal sash but is almost inappropriate in such a context. You can often judge the true quality of a football club from their own song. So any club whose anthem was originally sung by Marie Osmond pretty much is accepting that they are on one of the lower rungs of the ladder. I am not sure if you have ever heard "Paper Roses" but I would not advise it unless you are under the influence of lots of alcohol and/or heavy prescription drugs. It comes with its very own health warning as it is absolute dross so please be very careful.

Also their closest rivals are Ayr United and so these two heavyweights contest the less than impressive-sounding Ayrshire derby. It may well have been contested over 250 times but it has never quite made in on to the radar of Top 1,000 classic derbies, or on to many people's bucket lists as a must-see fixture. Ayr United have rarely troubled the top division and the last time they were it was twenty years ago so it has been a fair while since the two have locked horns at league level. Strangely Ayr United consider their biggest rivals to be Clydebank rather than Kilmarnock. As Clydebank disappeared off the face of this earth in 2002 (when they were swallowed up by Airdrie) and like similar phoenix clubs, have had to start again from the bottom that says quite a lot about the magnitude of the Ayrshire derby. Tinpot would be one of the milder descriptions.

Like so many clubs Kilmarnock have had issues with their board and dastardly owners but there is something especially sinister about this lot and in particular ex-chairman and company secretary and current owner Michael Johnston. Any fool knows that an army marches on its stomach and woe betide anybody who messes with a club's food provisions. Johnston inspired the wrath of much of the fan base with the decision to end the club's relationship with local bakery Browning's who were responsible for producing the celebrated 'Killie Pie'. With one of the few positive aspects of the club removed at a stroke there is really not much left to rescue the club's image. The dispute focused on who held the trademark for the 'Killie Pie' and managing director of Browning's John Gall summed up the whole farrago in April 2016. "I'm disappointed. I am a supporter of the club and I have put over £1 million into it over the years. But they made their position clear and there is no way back so I won't be supplying them with pies next season." So with that Kilmarnock effectively sealed their fate as once the catering has gone so has the club's entire reputation.

Perhaps one day this antipathy will change but all the signs are that this is now pretty much set for lifetime. I cannot imagine much altering but if I do end up making the trip to Rugby Park I may be pleasantly surprised by the whole occasion but for the moment I will be sticking to my guns that are firmly fixed on Killie as wrong 'uns.

Please do not take it personally good folk of Kilmarnock, it is just one of those strange quirks of fate and no harm is intended.

LASER PENS

It's very clear, they're not allowed and we don't want to see them. It's common for us to open disciplinary cases for lasers. It depends on what other incidents happen during the game, we put them all together, but a wide range of measures can be taken. It's up to the club and the police to control what fans bring into the stadium, but the club are responsible for the behaviour of their fans during matches.

UEFA statement from 2013

Whoever first thought of the idea of taking a laser pen to a football match needs to be sectioned. There is no earthly reason why any sane human being would indulge in shining a light into a player's eyes unless they are training to be an ophthalmic surgeon on the side. It simply defies belief. I am not absolutely sure what the main purpose of a laser pen is but I am pretty sure distracting a footballer is not included in the key features on the box.

I suspect they first came about in James Bond spy sets along with invisible ink and suicide pellets but I am pretty sure that nobody is packing those items as part of their essential kit before setting off for a match just yet. Quite how they made the journey to football grounds is beyond me, but they certainly have done. As these will be the same people who get their kicks out of shining their pens at aircraft overhead there can be little sense drilled into them as they are clearly brainless or psychopaths or possibly both. I am also a little unsure what the legitimate use of laser pens might entail but whatever it is it is not going to warrant their existence.

Don't get me wrong I'm all for diversionary tactics and for making the most of home advantage. There is an unwritten rule that this is perfectly acceptable as long as it is confined to the John Beck school of cold showers and under-inflated practice balls. I once overheard the ball boys at Selhurst Park being given a pre-match briefing when they were told to slow down the retrieval and delivery of the ball if the home side were leading so anything goes. And we all remember the spat involving Eden Hazard and the Swansea ball boy, which led to the Belgian's dismissal for trying to wrestle the ball away from underneath his not inconsiderable body.

That is not subterfuge but good old-fashioned one-upmanship and there is always a place for that in football. However, this move into the world of espionage is really a step too far. The last thing we need is something that would come out of a John Le Carre book sneaking into football. Next thing we know we will have Tom Hiddleston in the stands giving it the large one as he waves his laser pen into the air and we know where that will end. That's correct, a lavish BBC six-part series to be broadcast on Sunday evenings.

I also have found it hard to fathom why the beam is always green, surely there should be an array of colours to choose from if you are aiming to temporarily blind somebody shouldn't there? I mean what is wrong with mauve or orange. I am sure the good folks over at Nike could offer some invaluable help and guidance in this matter [See B for Balls]. Surely the technology exists to offer a little bit of technicoloured variety. Apparently, my research team have reliably informed me that there is a red version but the green ones are up to 50 times stronger and more likely to inflict damage. So green it is then.

One of the first reported incidents that led to some action was back in March 2008 when Cristiano Ronaldo was still strutting his stuff for Manchester United. In a Champions League at the Stade Gerland in Lyon, Ronaldo was targeted several times both during the pre-match warm-up and the game itself and the home club were fined a rather odd and paltry amount of £2,520. There is also the small issue of health here as having these things beams directed straight into your eyes cannot be much good for ones vision. Perhaps the laser pen has become the modern equivalent of the toilet roll that used to be hurled from the terraces to distract the player on the ball.

Such incidents have been going on for a while now and this dastardly intrusion reached such a level that even UEFA were forced to step and make an official statement back in 2013, as quoted in the introduction to this chapter. When it is clear to the good folks at UEFA you know we have a massive problem on our hands. So that is pretty unequivocal, even UEFA is anti-laser pens, as one must assume is FIFA. Maybe as FIFA disbanded their anti-racism task force after they had "completely fulfilled its temporary mission" they could be redeployed to rid the game of a few other ills of the game including laser pens. After all they are on a bit of a roll so why not, these things are usually about momentum and they are now in a place to sweep all before them. As soon as that FIFA sub-committee is up and running the problems with laser pens will go up in a plume of (green) smoke. Job done, mission accomplished and, as they are so fond of saying in football circles, on to the next one whatever that might be.

A piece of writing or other content presented wholly or partially in the form of a list: a recent BuzzFeed listicle called 21 Pictures That Will Restore Your Faith in Humanity has attracted more than 13 million views.

From Oxford English Living Dictionary

Now I appreciate that I may be coming across as slightly hypocritical here as somebody who has compiled and is compiling a book based around the A-Z format. However, in my defence I am not against lists per se, and some of my closest friends are lists, but there are lists and then there are lists. My ire is directed towards those lists, which make absolutely no sense that are continuously churned out with no thought. I will give you a few examples so you understand where I draw the line.

The very fact that these are known in some quarters as listicles sums up their worth. Listicles for Christ's sake. Just the word itself makes any sane person shudder and there is no way that anyone in their right mind would even consider this as remotely acceptable. Even more irritatingly, there are lots of sub genres of these infernal things and they seem to just mutate and multiply. There seems to be no stopping their exponential growth as this new breed of journalisticles (sic) make themselves heard above the noise of people screaming in horror.

The first one is that staple of nearly every media outlet the Five Things You Don't Know About X formula. It is the delusion of the writer to actually imagine anyone would be in any way interested. In the first place we usually do not know those five things precisely because we do not actually care two hoots about the subject in question. Such as Five Things You Don't Know About Rochdale's away form. This sort of list is only of interest to diehard Rochdale fans and usually those things are already known by the Spotland cognoscenti so are of little use to them or anybody else for that matter. Maybe the only person who may spark any curiosity out of is Jeff Stelling as one of those nuggets that he is so fond of divulging whilst in full flow on a Saturday afternoon.

We move from this relatively harmless list to a far more dangerous being – Five Things You NEED to Know About X. Here the so-called writer is sending out a challenge to each and every one of us. So valuable are these five things that your life will be improved immeasurably by reading about them. This information is going to improve your self-esteem and probably secure you that date with the very apple of your eye that you have been yearning after this past year. So pay close attention or else that golden chance is gone forever.

Also what is this obsession with FIVE things what is wrong with four or even six, why is it always five for goodness sake? Yes it is a 'handy' number but does everything have to revert to the same number. Personally I do not think five is enough to make a convincing argument for anything. If there is something really worth saying then seven would surely be nearer the mark but clearly in the current environment seven would be way over the top. It is too much to expect the reader to keep attention all the way up to seven, as that is way beyond most people's powers of concentration. Stick to five, buddy, you know it makes sense. I have to admit I have fallen into this trap myself, encouraged by the publisher and I felt dirty and ashamed because of it. To plead the classic freelance amendment of doing pretty much anything for cash in straitened times does not really wash and I hated myself for this misdemeanour.

In the end the main problem is not with the number five, but in the formulaic way in which these pieces are put together, the first two points are generally blindingly obvious, the next two are borderline whilst the last one, the deal clincher is usually a little outrageous, a little left field thus leaving a lasting impression on the reader. Repeat and rinse. This leads us to the sort of anodyne football writing that barely adds any enlightenment but it generates a fair amount of heat, and as we all know from bitter experience the more heat the less light.

Then we have that staple of any football journalist worth his salt, not a list exactly but the much-venerated team sheet which they share with us an hour before kick-off. It is all so terribly intimate as the photo of the sheet is sent out via social media. It is almost as though you are in the press box with the great and good enjoying the fruits of the pre-match snacks or drinks and conversing with them about the prospects for the game ahead. Oh the sheer thrill of almost being there can be too much to bear.

Perhaps the very worst of this plague of lists are the pictorial ones that are visually so seductive but contain as much content as a very empty vessel indeed. If you get beyond the second one then you either have the patience of a saint or you have far too much time on your hands. This little exercise will take up at least half an hour of your time that could have better spent plucking the fluff out of your navel or clearing your ear wax with a couple of cotton buds.

The majority of these lists fall under the generic banner of clickbait, the collective noun for being duped into clicking on pages by sensational or provocative material. Punters are lured by the dangling of a juicy carrot, only to end up with a field of mouldy turnips. The sheer volume of football content has expanded at an exponential rate so we are awash with information, which is in some ways good but in other ways bad. There are many different routes to obtaining information and to put it mildly, not all routes are that productive with the majority of them ending up in cul-de-sacs of frustration.

What generally happens is that you find yourself innocently trawling through a search on a subject of personal or professional interest, such as a player or a club, when you alight on something that looks absolutely spot on and just what you are have been searching for. You then get dragged into the primordial swamp that quickly envelops you, leaving you desperate for air but seemingly not able to breathe.

There are several techniques employed to entrap the unwary and probably the most annoying one is that used by hundreds of local papers who are so desperate to cling on to your online presence that they throw all sorts of things at you as soon as you start scrolling down. The online survey is one that raises the hackles as it is not only cumbersome but also incredibly dull and time-consuming. Having been lured in by a headline that suggests your star striker is going to be out for a few weeks, you are being quizzed about your views of a new tramline opening in the next ten years.

You are soon enmeshed in a maze of non-sequiturs and cul-de-sacs that has your head spinning. A few short questions turn into a major exercise in self-restraint in not smashing the laptop, tablet or phone you are using into the nearest wall. Nobody gains from this whole charade as the reader is turned off the piece he was initially interested in, the paper alienates a member of its audience and the article remains unread beneath the rubble of the questionnaire. You never do find out about the striker's fitness, of more pressing concern is your own mental fitness to cope with the rage and turmoil that is gnawing away as a result of this not so merry dance.

Surely it makes sense to be absolutely upfront about this sort of thing and not to pull people under false pretences and there should be a warning of some sort to alert people of the dangers that lie ahead. The amount of time wasted is bordering on the criminal and you can chastise yourself as much as you like for falling into the same old trap but it happens again and again.

The one that usually gets me is the half-finished quote that is tantalising enough to overcome your inhibitions and prompt further investigation. But you know as soon as you do go any further where this will end up, with ads aplenty and no more content for a while. Persisting with this is likely to send you wild so it is advisable to bail out as soon as possible. There are some media outlets, which specialise in this terrible practice, in fact they do little else and certainly do not have any content worthy of its name. These pesky people are the modern equivalent of highwaymen who lure the unsuspecting into a trap before robbing them blind, but without the style or panache of a Dick Turpin. You can chastise yourself as many times as you wish but rest assured that you will be dragged kicking and screaming down that highway to hell.

So here is Marc Webber, journalist and broadcaster, who pops up on BBC Final Score most Saturdays, to elucidate on exactly what Clickbait is all about.

"You'll never believe what happened next!!" Well, yes I can actually. I will click on the link to your article which will supposedly enlighten me some revelatory moment in sport, and what will actually happen is I will be served a page with 15 adverts; rolling video with no sound muted and, eventually, a story which will either be a mash up of several tweets I've already read or a story I saw on the small column of a back page two weeks ago.

Sports clickbait, the biggest let down since discovering an empty Viagra packet at the time your missus suggests your luck is in. And it is all done for the sake of revenue generation. Whilst companies spend millions of pounds employing people to ensure their Google search ranking is high by loading their sites with relevant keywords, the sports industry has encouraged the creation of a number of clickbait sites where "stories" are created with the aim to amaze, but actually are just there as a way of creating easy revenue for chancers who have no desire to invest in original journalism. They are about as well informed on the story they publish as the two drunk guys that sit in the corner of your local.

Think of clickbait sites as the bastard child of SEO (Search Engine Optimisation) and the fake news sites that prevailed during the US elections. I could name a few such sites. But there is no point, because they might have changed their name twice by the time you read this and they would probably claim they are not clickbait, but wonderfully engaging and informative viral banter. But you can spot them a mile off.

The giveaway sign is the over the top yet inviting headline like "you'll never guess what happened next" or "amazing news about (insert sport star here)'s next mega move to a shock club". Anything written with an element of hyperbole on the football Internet should be instantly viewed as clickbait. Saying that, most headlines on even respected websites during the transfer window are laden with hyperbole; so it is best to hide away during that period and accept it as an exception to this rule.

The name says it all. It is designed to get you to click that headline. The headline only has one purpose. Now, in Ye Olden Days of the Internet, clickbait headlines would have been punished by the SEO police. Google bots would have had a hyperbole sensor and would have dismissed such headlines as an unworthy jumble of words.

However, SEO is irrelevant in this case as these headlines are made for the social media generation. As long as it has 140 characters and is eye grabbing, it works, because most of the traffic for clickbait sites comes from social sharing on Twitter or Facebook. If you are sharing headlines like this, you are enhancing the value of clickbait in football.

Secondly, look at the content. That is a clear giveaway the article is being created for profit. If the video is poor or scraped off YouTube or a vine, then the article is clickbait. If the words you are reading (or embedded tweets) are from a story you've already read in the paper a couple of days ago, it is clickbait.

But is there really any difference between clickbait and gossip stories found in newspapers? Or even the celebrity-laden picture drivel often found gracing the Mail Online site? Yes, there is. At least the pictures taken of celebrities and the stories written there are the fruits of some sort of journalistic endeavour. A paid journalist has taken those pictures or written those words, however banal they may seem. With clickbait, it is content scraped with no investment and rehashed by some unqualified web content writer in the name of Bantz. This person is unlikely to have done any formal qualification in journalism. And it's not even that. Their experience of football would largely have been watching the same viral content they are scraping. Even worse, there might not even be any humans involved in generating clickbait articles at all. It might even just be pulled together by a robot with no human effort, aside from the original tech development to make it.

Clickbait is dumbing down the conversation we are having about the sport we love. It is distracting us from having sensible conversations about players, teams and the rules by distracting us with wow-factor headlines to content, which adds nothing to those debates. In a time-poor world it is the content that reinforces invalid opinions and robs is of time to explore other beliefs or attitudes.

It is the fog that is creeping in over the coast that is stripping revenue from the genuine content creators, whether they are journalists or clubs or fans. Whilst clickbait sites spam you with programmatic advertising around content made by others, that money isn't going to the people that made the original product that appears on the page. For every video view of a club video or a fan video on a clickbait site, that site gets revenue. Does it pass any of that ad revenue back to the club or the fan that filmed it? Doubtful.

That's why a number of big clubs have got together recently to create a website called Dugout which aims to conquer clickbait sites using club content. Smaller clubs, of course, don't have that luxury. Thankfully, one of the sites that was considered king of the clickbait at one stage is now going "legit" and has set up its own content and sales arms to make genuine output and revenue. Time will tell if others follow suit.

Of course, like anything in a capitalist society, it only exists if there is a demand for it.

If people buy beer, there will always be breweries trying to create the best and cheapest ale around. If we all went teetotal, there would be no breweries.The same with clickbait. It only exists through need. People want to consume as much about their club, or football in general. So they gorge on whatever's out there. But consuming the football content equivalent of Tesco value baked beans ain't gonna make you a better fan. Like they used to advise those secretly recording songs on their home cassette machines in the 1970s – pirating is killing music, kids. Don't do it!

MUTUAL CONSENT

Except by mutual consent, a Club or Player is not entitled to determine an agreement between them without the written consent of the Football Association or in accordance with Rule C1(I).

From the FA Handbook relating to players

So now you know from this self-explanatory paragraph all is abundantly clear or is it? It is a phrase that is trotted out regularly when somebody parts company such as Sam Allardyce's departure from the England job. "The FA and Allardyce have mutually agreed to terminate his contract with immediate effect." Forgive me for any sense of cynicism over this but I very much doubt that when Allardyce was summoned to FA HQ at Wembley on the day those Telegraph 'pint of wine' revelations broke that both parties were in full accord on what should happen next. Even in the most harmonious of relationship break-ups the idea of mutual consent is a load of balderdash and is just Public Relations spin that is spiralling out of control and is barely credible.

Allardyce was clearly spitting feathers when the press caught up with him outside his Bolton home after what effectively was a dismissal. There was not much evidence of mutuality or consent in his statement. "Obviously I have to do this before I go away. On reflection it was a silly thing to do. I was trying to help somebody out I knew for 30 years and unfortunately it was an error in judgement on my behalf. Entrapment has won on this occasion." He was not a happy bunny and was not hiding the fact. One can only imagine the FA watching this statement and keeping fingers and toes crossed about how far he might go.

Under such circumstances there is always one side that feel that they have been hard done by and have come off appreciably worse. This notion of all concerned agreeing with the decision reached is patently laughable. You only have to look at Allardyce in this first public statement to see how he was seething with rage and looked fit to burst with indignation. Tellingly he then said that he could not say any more as he was bound by a confidentiality agreement and would not be answering any more questions, which was a pity because it would be have been interesting to hear somebody ask him how mutual that agreement was. The more's the pity we will probably never know for sure but we can take a damned good guess. Naturally the £1 million settlement that Allardyce was due to receive after the parting of the ways would have gone a long way to ensuring its mutuality on the surface.

When Jose Mourinho parted company with Chelsea in December 2015 the club gamely announced that it was by mutual consent but Mourinho had a rather different interpretation of events, which he revealed to Sky Sports. "Mr Abramovich decided to sack me. I left with not one bad word about anything or anyone at the club." To be fair he did not really need to say too much after the previous turbulent few months when the defending champions imploded. Firstly, he had already fallen out with his medical staff who were "naïve" and did not understand the game, leading to club doctor Eva Carneiro's messy and ultimately costly departure from the club.

Furthermore his players were openly castigated after the defeat to Leicester that hastened Mourinho's exit - "I feel my work is betrayed."

Mourinho could not have much clearer in that Sky Sports interview that when he left the second time round it was a one-way street and he even gave his previous departure from Stamford Bridge as a comparison to prove his point. "It was not mutual consent. That was in my first period at Chelsea when I agreed it was time to change. I was keen to change, more than ready to go to other countries but this time it was not like that." There you have it, from the horse's mouth, the crucial difference outlined between mutual consent and a good old sacking.

It feels as though nobody is willing to tell the truth and the main reason behind that is that the advice of lawyers, conscious of the cost of any falling out, ringing in their ears. Indeed the very idea of mutual consent must have been dreamed up and conceived by some legal boffin as nobody in the real world would use the words in such close proximity especially as the phrase is a tad tautological. The next time 'mutual consent' is used I can pretty much guarantee that there is nothing mutual about it and there will be very little consent either.

In another example of the vacuous nature of mutual consent I give you Tony Pulis' abrupt departure from Selhurst. When Pulis left Palace on the eve of the 2014/15 season there was widespread consternation amongst the fans as it left the Eagles, to put it mildly, up Shit Creek without a paddle. It was officially described at the time as by mutual consent but a year or so later that idea was well and truly blasted out of the water when the club successfully sued Pulis for considerable damages and the Welshman was ordered to pay back his £2 million for keeping Palace up, plus £1 million in damages and to top it all off a further £500,000 in legal costs. So if close to £4 million is the price of mutual consent I would hate to see what happens when people fall out.

Bayern Munich are a club that does things right, both on and off the pitch and they showed the way to cut through all this puffery and post-truth rationalisation nonsense when they released their official statement on the impending departure of Philipp Lahm, who decided to terminate his contract a year earlier than expected. After over twenty years' service as man and boy, 500 matches, many of which were as captain, an array of trophies, including just the eight Bundesliga championships, a Champions League and six DFB Cups, one would imagine Lahm had done enough to earn the respect of his club. But Bayern's chairman Karl-Heinz Rummenigge was clearly in no mood for empty platitudes as he let rip with both barrels in response to the news that he was off.

"FC Bayern is surprised by the approach of Philipp Lahm and his adviser. Uli Hoeness and I have held open, intensive and constructive talks with Philipp in recent months about a possible position as sporting director of our club. At the end of last week, he informed us that he is currently not available for such a position and that he would like an early termination of his player contract, which runs until June 2018. Until yesterday we assumed that there would be a joint announcement." How refreshing it is to read a statement with not a trace of mutual consent and to revel in the brutal light shed by unadorned honesty.

And fair play to Leicester City's vice chairman Aiyawatt Srivaddhanaprabha who avoided using the dreaded words when the axe finally landed on Claudio Ranieri's neck in February 2017. True, the unwavering support of a few weeks beforehand was not too much in evidence as the manager who delivered the most unlikely and unexpected top flight championship was jettisoned within nine months of that historic, never to be repeated success. It was clear from the official statement that this was a tough decision "we are duty-bound to put the Club's long-term interests above all sense of personal sentiment, no matter how strong that might be." Brutal yes but at least they did not resort to the mealy-mouthed refuge that is mutual consent.

NUMBERS ON SHIRTS

Brazilian fourth-tier side Fluminense de Feira have taken shirt sponsorship to a whole new level. Not content with simply featuring sponsor's logos on their shorts as well as their shirts, the Brasileiro Série D side have started using their shirt numbers to advertise special offers in the local supermarket. Players now have a product written where their name would usually be printed on the back of their shirts, with conventional numbers replaced with the prices of bargain deals.

From the Independent 7 April 2017

Stuart Fuller is modern football's Renaissance Man in that he does pretty much everything that anyone connected with football has ever done but he manages somehow to do all of it in just over a week when it takes mere mortals usually a lifetime. He has been to over 700 different grounds in 84 countries. He is a stable mate of mine at Ockley Books, which is lovely but problem is that he makes me and the other Ockley authors look like indolent slackers with no interest in or passion for the game. Damn your eyes, Fuller. So here's our Man For All Seasons, Mr Stuart Fuller on shirt numbers:

My niggle is about how numbers are put on the back of shirts not the actual number itself. I don't really care about the numbering system used, although my alternative suggestion to a penalty shoot out to determine the winner of drawn cup games of awarding the game to the team with the lowest average shirt number of the players on the pitch still hasn't been acknowledged by FIFA.

I'm talking about the decision by clubs and kit manufacturers but put gold numbering on the back of white shirts, or white numbers on black striped ones. Picture the scene. It's a cold, blustery November midweek game. The floodlights barely create a shadow on the pitch. You are positioned 100 yards away at the far end of the ground and in a goal-mouth melee the ball hits the back of the net. Alas with the away team sporting white shirts with gold numbers on the back. Why should I care? Well in this instance I hold the microphone to announce such info.

"Oi! Keeper. Who scored?" In this instance the goalie falls in the 50% bracket of being billy big bollocks and not acknowledging there's a hundred or so fans behind him.

I move down to the edge of the pitch and wave the microphone in his direction, the international symbol for "speak to me". Still no answer. By now the players have returned to their starting positions. The crowd of 300 wait expectantly for my announcement. I'm forced to go round to the dug outs. Again, a wall of silence. Our kit man sees my frustration and has a word with their kit man and I have my answer. Goal announced, the internet becomes aware and player X's strike goes down in history.

Alas, the internet sometimes isn't forgiving and within a few minutes I'm directed to a written 140 character tirade aimed at me, via the club's official account, because I'd got the scorer wrong. It wasn't player X but actually player Y who got the slightest of touches to the already goal-bound strike I'm reliably informed by Mrs Y, who I assume based on the youthful looks of Player Y, is his Mum. Non-League lesson number 73 - never upset a player's Mum. We correct the score on the internet but I decide not to make a correcting announcement for the 3 or 4 away fans who already know the correct scorer thanks to Mrs Y's verbal rant on the opposite terrace.

I reply to the tweet with an apology and point out the issues with the yellow numbers but she's having none of it. Alas, video replays are rarely made available to us down at step 8 of the Non-League pyramid. However, clubs all have the opportunity to consider the impact of their shirt numbering strategy.

It's not just down in the grass-roots the problem exists. Fortunately, the quality of the floodlights in the professional game make it easier to see the numbers but that didn't stop Newcastle United putting gold letters on the back of a black and white striped shirt a few years ago that had the likes of Alan Green complaining about his eyesight.

So my plea to clubs is to think about the poor PA announcer who has a tough job as it is having to concentrate for 90 minutes without taking a comfort break (guilty), going to the bar (very guilty) or simply forgetting they have the microphone (all the time) to have to also deal with poor numbers.

A letter addressed to a particular person or group of people but intended for publication in a newspaper or journal.

Definition of an open letter, Oxford Living Dictionaries – source?

In these days of instant messaging it may be instructive to remind ourselves about the rationale behind that traditional form of communication, the letter. In the trusty OED a letter is defined as 'a written, typed or printed communication, usually sent by post or messenger.' The very idea of a letter is that it is specifically and directly targeted at somebody thus the idea of an open letter is contrary to the principle as its purpose is to give everybody the chance to pry into the affairs between the two correspondents.

In a political context open letters do have credence because the writer of the letter is trying to raise public awareness of a key issue or major concern. It is when football players get hold of the open letter that we encounter problems aplenty. In the same way as genuine sandwiches by definition can never be truly open, then neither should letters from footballers. One has to question why anyone would want to make this public but then when you look into the recent history of open letters all becomes abundantly clear.

We have experienced a glut of players who wrote heart-rending pieces to their millions of adoring fans about why they were leaving their club or offering an explanation of some error of judgement. Funnily enough not one of those mentioned a better deal or more money; there were either extenuating circumstances or personal issues but never was it a financial consideration. Of course it wasn't. It is all about the deep love and respect that the player has for those who have been paying his wages but who he is now having to say a fond farewell.

Samuel Eto'o was so pleased with his heart-rending farewell message to Everton in early 2015 that he felt it was worthy of repetition. He must have had Blue Noses everywhere choking with emotion as the Cameroonian international kicked off his valedictory message with "Dear Toffees, I've been blessed to spend these past few months with you," and then signed off "It was an honour to be part of your army.

You will always be in my heart." There was not a dry eye in the house of Goodison as he departed for Sampdoria.

Then fast forward to July and Eto'o was leaving Sampdoria so it was time to gather up the emotional baggage again "Dear Blucerchiati, I've been blessed to spend these past few months with you," and the letter continued not just in the same vein but pretty much word for word and with that killer line "It was an honour to be part of your army. You will always be in my heart." Well the conclusion to all this parallel outpouring of emotion is that Samuel must have a massive heart with so many people taking up residence. Just one small point though, copy and pasting your innermost, candid thoughts and feelings is not well suited to the forum of an open letter, better to keep those to private correspondence because there is less chance of being rumbled as a fraud.

Angel Di Maria is also clearly a man of letters and quite prolific when it comes to leaving. He wrote one when he left Real Madrid for Manchester United and was at it again a year later when he was off to Paris St. Germain after an unhappy stay at Old Trafford. "When Manchester United chose me as the part of their team, I felt extremely honoured because I knew what this club means and how it trusted me." It is enough to make one weep. The other essential element of the open letter, which Di Maria has perfected, is shown in all its glory right here - "Also a special mention to all the fans who always trusted me and showed me their respect and love." Well done Angel old boy, respect and love are indeed absolute fundamentals, throw in the fans and Bingo you have completed the set.

This seems more of a vanity project than a genuine appeal to the fans where the Argentine is intent on covering his arse just in case the fans think he is a wrong 'un. After leaving United I wonder how much time Di Maria really spent thinking about those he had left behind as he sipped a coffee in a Parisian cafe. Another seasoned exponent of the open letter also ended up at PSG, the upwardly mobile Hatem Ben Arfa. He is undoubtedly a hugely talented player who just cannot seem to settle down and expressed his feelings when moving from Newcastle to Hull on loan. He started his letter strongly "To the Toon Army" and continued in a similar vein when explaining how the fans would be "forever in my heart." Then he finished with a flourish that will ensure a warm welcome on Tyneside if he ever returns by signing off "Howay the Lads."

Then there was that scion of moral rectitude Stan Collymore, who decided it was time to offer young Villa whippersnapper Jack

Grealish some of his worldly advice. As Grealish had been spending more time on the front pages of the newspapers than the back pages after yet another late night jaunt Collymore offered these sage words. "Anyone who says 'You're only young once, fuck them, it's only fun', they are the ones, whoever they are, who need to go in the bin."

Collymore who suffered from plenty of hangers-on during his career has a point and it is a good one but one wonders why this could not have been communicated between just the two of them and not in the glare of publicity.

The idea of a quiet word in the ear has clearly lost its appeal and has been replaced by the loud word blasted across the wide, open spaces of social media. Does this help or hinder a flawed individual who clearly has issues? The suspicion is that this form of communication is chosen because it also raises the profile of the person sending it as much as it helps the recipient. And so there may be another agenda beyond the ostensible reason of helping out a fellow professional. It is not just the players who are culpable of such questionable behaviour even chairmen are at it as well. As somebody once pointed out the fish rots from the head.

After their wretched 2015/16 season Villa fans should really be spared this final indignity but step forward Steve Hollis. After their inevitable relegation was finally sealed after a 1-0 loss at Old Trafford the Villa chairman Hollis decided it was time to speak. "We must acknowledge that this weekend's confirmation has been the culmination of an unacceptably fractured season both on and off the pitch." Well I have heard it called many things in my lifetime of watching football but to describe the utter bilge that the Villa Park faithful had to put up with week in week out as "unacceptably fractured" is really taking the biscuit. That makes it sound as though there was something vaguely positive lurking underneath the surface, which just went a little bit awry. But that most certainly was not the case and there was nothing there apart from what we would traditionally call a complete bunch of old shite.

Then, of course there was Steven Gerrard's departure from LA Galaxy after 18 months' hard work at the StubHub Center (sic). You may recognise some of this last paragraph. "Los Angeles will always have a special place in my heart. As I depart, I want to thank everyone at the club for making my time here so memorable for me and my family. Thank you and go Galaxy." Now he was doing so well, following a well-worn, formulaic path until that last line when he really let the side down and veered into dangerous waters. For a man who has been cruelly lambasted for his 'slip' this is further evidence that he is still falling. Still he heads towards it almost oblivious of the danger he is hurtling towards at an almighty lick. I am tempted to say go Stevie G but have managed to resist.

Even blighted chairmen have succumbed to the idea. Fawaz Al Hasawi has not exactly been flavour of the month at the City Ground as a team that once won two European Cups in swift succession had become marooned in the Championship under Hasawi and have become more concerned with dropping into League One than challenging to return to the Premier League. The chairman decided to reassure the fans of "my complete and utter commitment to Nottingham Forest and securing its long-term position as a thriving and successful club – both on and off the pitch."

It is just as well that Hasawi got this out in the open over the last few years you would be hard pressed to see any evidence of anything positive and having rattled through a handful of managers in that time as results have declined so that rather than thriving and successful, deteriorating and hapless might be more apposite adjectives. Still now they have read this open letter no doubt the Forest faithful will suddenly be of sunny disposition as everything is alright on the banks of the Trent. When Hasawi finally shuffled off into the distance there were not many tears shed by the Trent.

And so in the spirit of research and in trying to fathom out why anybody in their right mind would be tempted to do so, here is my very own open letter to all those considering writing one in the near future.

TO WHOM IT MAY CONCERN

This letter is offered as a friendly piece of advice. Just take a little time to consider what the impact of your letter might be. You need to question whether it is really in the public interest to air your thoughts on this subject. Be honest with yourself when judging what the prime motivation is behind this. If it is to address a particular issue then is this the best way to do that or is there some other form of communication, which would better serve your purpose? Think carefully about the consequences for both yourself but more importantly the person to whom the letter is addressed.

I am sure you have heard the proverb 'Do not wash your dirty linen in public.' That is pretty sound advice because nobody benefits when things are broadcast that do not warrant an audience that is broader than the person/s you are writing to. Indeed this can often lead to more questions being asked than is strictly necessary and can often draw attention to something that the other person would much rather keep to themselves and for good reason.

An open letter should always be the last resort and not a knee jerk response to a situation, so only use if you have truly exhausted all the possible alternatives and then think again seriously before doing it. There are only very few occasions where you should send an open letter so the default position should be no, not on my life.

And finally, if you are still contemplating sending an open letter just remember how you felt when you read one and bear in mind all that anger, frustration and the generally negative reaction that it generated. Is this what you want to achieve? No we thought not, so it is now time to move on and find another way of expressing yourself because the case for an open letter of any shape, size or colour is closed and will remain firmly shut for the rest of time.

Over and out.

Yours faithfully.

All football fans

PROTESTS BY FANS

It is the nature of a man as he grows older – to protest against change, particularly changes for the better.

John Steinbeck, American writer

One of the most interesting and positive developments of the last few years has been the increasingly powerful voice of the fans, as represented by organisations such as Football Supporters Federation and Supporters Direct. Rogue owners are quite rightly called to account and issues such as fairer ticket pricing at the top end of the game have seen some action taken so all power to these organisations' and the fans whom they represent. However, there is still a long way to go before striking the proper balance in the power struggle between the authorities, owners and the long-suffering fans.

I am all for fans expressing their disgust at their own club's ineptitude. We have all been there when the same mistakes are being made week in week out and it drives you nuts. Seemingly everybody can see it apart from the people making decisions at the club, such as playing an emergency left back who has no left foot, or the striker who has only a passing acquaintance with the idea of scoring a goal. We feel utterly powerless when frustration turns into blind rage as watching becomes not just a chore but actually an embarrassment. It all gets a bit too much for the soul to bear and so some sort of release of all this pent-up emotion is required.

It is all part of the cathartic process that following a football club entails. If you cannot rant and rave at the shortcomings of your team then there is something amiss in the world. And as many eminent sociologists have proved beyond reasonable doubt this process actually helps us all let off steam that would otherwise be directed at loved ones and cause far more damage to our lives. It is far better to howl derision at the manager or the players than at your partner or your children.

So far so good but what troubles me is not that this happens or even the strength of feeling that is often bordering on the psychotic, but it is the manner of the protests that has raised some serious concerns. I have no issue with a spontaneous outburst giving the manager dog's abuse for dropping yet another tactical clanger that seals yet another humiliating defeat, and even the occasional chant of "You don't know what you're doing" is acceptable or in extremis "you're not fit to wear the shirt". It is the over-orchestrated protests that rankle, the ones where the focus switches on the protestors rather than those against whom they are protesting. It's when those protestors come across as a sad, sorry collection of sanctimonious moaners and whingers that the concerns start to build.

One of the more ridiculous I have witnessed was at Selhurst Park many years ago but it is one that I have seen repeated across the country and the ludicrous nature of it does not diminish with every repetition. The match was towards the end of the 2000/2001 season and it was a thoroughly miserable affair, played in pouring rain that ended in a 2-0 defeat despite Wolves being reduced to 10 men for the whole of the second half. As the BBC summed it up cheerily "Crystal Palace are on the brink of relegation after another miserable defeat at Selhurst Park."

Alan Smith was the manager at the time and the fans turned on him with some venom as slipping into the third tier looked a certainty with only two away games remaining and anything less than six points probably spelling relegation. Amongst all the usual vitriol and fury one fan's course of action stood out for me and I couldn't help but laugh at the absurdity of it. This guy who had been sitting in the main stand just behind the managers' dug-outs, was giving as good as he got. As Smith sheepishly rose up after the full time whistle he was clearly keen to get to the tunnel as quickly as possible to avoid too much abuse that he knew would be directed at him.

Spotting Smith's hasty exit plan the fan in question was just drawing breath before he could bellow more insults at the beleaguered manager when suddenly an idea struck him about how to escalate this. He ran to the front of the stand to a spot not too far away from where Cantona launched his infamous kung fu-kick at Matthew Simmons in 1995 and then revealed his master plan. He took his season ticket out of his pocket, and encased in its plastic wallet he hurled it at Smith. When others saw what he had done they joined in so it was soon raining season tickets, most of which ended up forlornly scattered around the mud-splattered touchline.

Whilst the symbolism was both significant and pertinent there was a degree of emptiness about this particular protest, which suddenly dawned on me and this is when I started to laugh at the absurdity of it all. As this was the last home game of the season the sacrifice of one's season ticket is not in reality that much of a deal. The season ticket itself was at that point worthless and the only thing of value was the tatty plastic cover that would roughly have cost £2.35 at most. Anyway the fan must have got his point across to the club owner Simon Jordan as Smith was sacked that evening although how much influence the throwing of the redundant season ticket had on Jordan's decision. Improbably Palace survived by winning their last two games at Portsmouth and Stockport under caretaker manager Steve Kember.

If recently-expired season tickets flying through the air is not your thing then there are certainly other airborne forms of protest that could rival them and they are certainly on a grander scale. But these take over-elaboration on to an entirely new scale. They are the plane protests and they have become increasingly common. There was the rather ludicrous example set by Arsenal fans when they took on West Brom away in March 2017 as the rising resentment against the club's most successful manager (sic) reached boiling point; there was not one plane at it but two planes circling the Hawthorns with contradictory messages. One suggested that Wenger should leave – No Contract #Wenger Out screamed the first one while the other insisted that he should really be above all this sort of thing after twenty years at the helm – In Arsene We Trust #RespectAW. If there had been a good old-fashioned dogfight between the two planes then that maybe could have justified this over the top reaction. But it was left to the crass headline department to really sum up the state of affairs. Plane daft. So the 3-1 loss that they suffered on the pitch was suitable punishment for the antics of the latter day Red Barons as they jousted in the skies above.

One of the more memorable of its kind surfaced during the end of David Moyes' troubled and tortured managerial stint with Manchester United. The faltering form of the team that Ferguson built was clearly getting to United fans who had been fed on a diet of almost continuous success for well over twenty years. Come March 2014 it had dawned on many United supporters that this transition from one Scot to another was not going as smoothly as had been hoped and with the team already out of the race for the Premier League title, this was time to grab the bull by the horns. Compared to the Ferguson's last season when at the same point in the season they were 12 clear of Man City, this time they were 15 points behind and so the fans responded in the only way they could - by hiring a plane to lug a message of no-support over Old Trafford.

Step forward protest organiser Wes Anderson who in a BBC interview explained the rationale behind it. "The rumblings of discontent have started in the stands." [Where they should have stayed]. "We wanted to show that support isn't at 100% as Moyes would like to think," Anderson continued and in my mind he stepped a little too far. There have been plenty of precedents for this aeronautical angst, for example in the early 1980s, at Luton of all places, one of the original plane protests was held against the idea of moving to Milton Keynes long before the Wimbledon saga had begun.

This was one of the first times that a plane had been used as a form of protest in English football, but alas it certainly was not to be the last.

Generally the messages dragged behind planes are confined to those that fly over beach resorts with enticing messages along the lines of "Come to Joe's BBQ – All the Meat you can Eat for £10 up to 7pm tonight!" But this was supplanted by the pithy "Wrong One – Moyes Out" message that was emblazoned in seven-foot high red lettering and dragged across the skies above Old Trafford. There was no ignoring it but the majority of the Old Trafford crowd were not too enamoured by the anti-Moyes sentiment and either booed the plane or sang their support of Moyes. As United beat Villa 4-1 on the day, Moyes must have felt that things were beginning to turn round for him. However, that did not last and within a month Moyes had been dismissed. So maybe that protest did have its effect just as the old season ticket chucking at Selhurst had.

Six months after the United Villa game an altogether more worrying airborne protest took place. The first serious outbreak of a drone being used at a match was during the highly-charged European qualifying match between Serbia and Albania in Belgrade when a disgruntled Albanian fan decided that flying an Albanian flag incorporating Serbia would spice things up. He was not wrong as the Serbian players hauled the flag down and tore it up which sparked a mini riot amongst the players and then the fans and the odd security guard decided to join in. Cue the game being suspended and Albania being awarded the match 3-0, which ultimately helped them qualify for their first ever major championships at Euros in 2016.

With such a landmark victory the logical extension of this is that there will soon be a whole rash of drone protests as fans cotton on to the notion of a potentially season-saving tactic being in the palm of their hands. If your shaky defence cannot repel the opposition maybe that drone might do the job. Going airborne now seems to be the choice of these vocal protestors whether it be planes or drones. But alongside these there is the worrying medium, which is very much grounded is that of fans' petitions.

Petitions are another way of voicing their disapproval and there have been many that are fully justified such as FSF's Twenty's Plenty campaign that aimed to bring down admission prices for away fans, but quite often the subject matter is bordering on the frivolous. So there have been petitions to reverse controversial decisions made in a match, which is possibly the definition of pissing in the wind as the idea of changing things retrospectively is so far from reality that it is not of this world. Quite often these wails in the night are launched via bona fide organisations such as change.org, which give them some air of respectability they do not really merit.

These can get quite personal in their avowed target. When nearly 20,000 sign up to a petition to stop a player being picked in the England squad because "further embarrassment could be avoided by not having his inept performances undermine the rest of the team's efforts." Now I am no fan of Tom Cleverly but that is just plain vindictive. Poor old Tom. Before the idea of petitions this anti-Cleverly movement would have been centred on a few moans and groans in some post-match conversations but would not have delivered such a public humiliation. Those that argue that footballers are paid big bucks and should be able to accept such criticism are missing the point. It does not matter a jot how well you are remunerated when you have to withstand such low blows to your own dignity and self-respect.

However, other targets are more justified such as Michael Owen's less than dynamic and enlightening co-commentating or referee Mike Dean's continuing insistence on putting himself at the forefront of the action to the detriment of the players. But do we really need a petition to express any dissension? Perhaps the clearest indication of the futility of petitions was when Leeds fans summoned up one for the Football League to be persuaded to not oust Massimo Cellino from their club. Only a few months later this show of solidarity turned to a wave of protests against the Italian, including, you guessed it, a plane fly-by replete with their 'Time to Go' banner. And so everything had come full circle at Elland Road and potentially we reached the nadir of fans' protests. Maybe they should have tried an open letter to achieve the unholy trinity.

We can't promise it will happen now but eventually it will have to happen. We are the players at the moment who have been chosen to do it. If it's not us then it will be other players. This club definitely has a target to win every competition.

Vincent Kompany, Manchester City captain in 2014

I like Vincent Kompany and I think he is a classy footballer and an intelligent guy but I am afraid he is way wide of the mark about this. It is the impossible dream. There is a belief that one day a team is going to do it and take a clean sweep of every single trophy available – Premier League, FA Cup, League Cup and Champions League, aka the Quadruple. The only thing is that this is never going to happen but that does not stop the speculation. Even massive clubs such as Manchester City do not have the resources to challenge on four separate fronts but still The Quadruple gets raised as soon as a team gets past the first few rounds of the various Cups, the phantom image is conjured up like a modern Holy Grail and it is as elusive as its ancestor. The only quadruples that any footballers will ever get near to them realistically will be those being dispensed by a vodka luge.

The man we have to blame for all this is Sir Alex Ferguson who way back in 1999 achieved the one and only treble in British football. By setting the bar that little bit higher than previously, an expectation was then created that the next logical step would be the Quadruple. But let's bear in mind how difficult Ferguson's treble was to achieve. This was certainly not plain sailing and there were several 'squeaky bum' moments during the ultimately triumphant trilogy and nobody has really come close to emulating this since. Let's face it only a few teams have even managed to achieve the double so to expect others to double that achievement is stretching it a bit.

If ever a team was going to achieve a clean sweep it was Ferguson's United who were in the middle of their golden age. But even in this most dominant period all three elements had their hairy moments when they were a whisker away from falling at that particular hurdle. United were an injury time penalty save away from a FA Cup semi-final exit and needed not only Peter Schmeichel's penalty save at the end of 90 minutes but also Ryan Giggs' extraordinary goal in extra time to win it. The Premier League was only secured on the last day of the season after coming back from being a goal down to Tottenham and ultimately they won it by the slender margin of a single point from Arsenal. Then of course there was the small matter of the Champions League Final when they had to rely on those ever so late goals from SAS Mark II – Solskjaer and Sheringham – against Bayern Munich.

This was the zenith of Ferguson's 27-year reign at Old Trafford and the fact that this was all close to collapsing at so many crucial junctures suggests that adding another trophy to the pile is pretty much mission impossible. Their one failing that season was a 3-1 quarter-final defeat to Tottenham in the League Cup. This was also the time when United's only serious challenger on the domestic front were Arsenal whereas now there are a handful of clubs vying for top spot, all replete with endless reserves of cash, a hugely talented group of players and the smartest coaches from around the world. Regardless of this, the talk of the Quadruple shows no signs of abating.

It is the very nature of the fourth trophy that mitigates against it being added to the cabinet, nestling up against the other three.

The League Cup has been through more identity changes than a schizophrenic chameleon, which underlines that this is very much a lesser competition and this is where the heart of the problem lies. Even huge squads packed to the rafters with internationals reach a point when there is just one game too many. That match will be away to Norwich City on a chilly Tuesday November night in the Capital One Cup or the Tin Pot trophy or whatever it is called that month.

The influx of foreign coaches has also exacerbated the problem. When Ferguson started his United career in the 1986/87 season all the 22 managers in the First Division were British/Irish and Everton won the title under Howard Kendall, one of the last English managers to do so. At the start of the 2016/17 season there were only seven British managers in charge and none of those were realistically going to be jostling for position at the top of the league. The highest-placed British manager was Eddie Howe who took Bournemouth to the giddy heights of 9th, just the 47 points behind Chelsea. It is unlikely that stellar names such as Jurgen Klopp, Pep Guardiola and Antonio Conte ever dreamed of EFL Cup glory when they were growing up and as such it will hardly register on their list of priorities.

As Guardiola could frequently carry off all the domestic cups with Barcelona whilst having his hands tied behind his back, blindfolded and dangled upside down in a vat of honey, the task of adding the Champions League was a more singular and achievable objective. With no equivalent of that tricky midweek trip to Carrow Road to throw a spanner in the works, the smooth passage to domestic dominance would centre on their annual struggle with Real Madrid to share the spoils. When reaching the latter stages of the League Cup there may be a slight quickening of the pulse but that this coincides with when the Champions League begins to get serious and moves into the knockout phase, meaning a choice has to be made and there are no prizes for guessing which takes precedence.

For the ultimate proof of how unattainable and impossible the Quadruple is there is only one man who is qualified to comment. In 2010 Ferguson said that "You don't win everything, of course, but you try." However, the final words must rest with Guardiola when he was asked about the likelihood of the Quadruple at a press conference in September 2016 after setting the record of eight consecutive wins in all competitions for a new Manchester City manager. He just shook his head and muttered under his breath but quite audibly "What the fuck?" followed by a protracted silence and more head shaking. Exactly, Pep, exactly.

Whilst we all appreciate that Guardiola has an excellent football brain, the fact is it took him only a few weeks to work out that this Quadruple was impossible, so why everybody else insists on raising the idea is unfathomable. But still at the start of every season there will be the question posed to an unsuspecting manager after winning a couple of games. They might as well ask some less unrealistic questions such as do you think England can win the next World Cup or are Hartlepool going to win the Champions league in the next five years or will the FA's Wembley debt ever be paid off?

RETIREMENT (FALSE)

I am very grateful [to return to the national team]. But I did not deceive anybody when I retired, I felt that. We were very disappointed with what had happened, but after that I thought better.

Lionel Messi on his return to the Argentina team in September 2016, having quit in June 2016 after Copa America defeat to Chile.

Messi's retirement lasted no more than three months and although he is untouchable as a player one has to suspect his motives behind that original exit. When sportspeople retire they are accorded due reverence, particularly after a long and illustrious career. We can all recognise that they cannot go on forever as their bodies begin to show the inevitable signs of wear and tear from so many physical demands. However, there are retirements and there are retirements. The ones that get to me are those announcements that as soon as they are made you know deep down that they are not really genuine. Most of these involve calling it a day on appearing for their country under the umbrella of international retirement. The players are still going to turn out for their clubs, who after all is said and done, pay their salaries but they have decided to hang up their boots for their country. Scott Brown, are you hearing me?

When everyone's favourite Rottweiler/ Midfield Enforcer/ Braveheart Extra/ Trainspotting Extra/ Captain Courageous announced he was hanging up his sharply studded boots the outpouring of grief and relief from all the great football nations was cacophonous. How could such a scion of the game, a master of the pitch be depriving the world stage of such a talent? But it was true the Dunfermline Destroyer who graced Easter Road before moving to Champions-elect Celtic in 2007 decided in the summer of 2016 that he would join his ancestors Dalglish, Law and Strachan on the sidelines.

But wait look what happened a few months later and coincidentally just before the jolly old England Scotland tear-up aka World Cup Qualifier at Wembley, Brown was back on his white charger to rescue the Scots as they faltered in fourth place in the Group of Life with football giants such as Malta, Lithuania and Slovenia. So back he came and the returning hero was made captain naturally. Some seven months down the line and after the 2-2 draw with the Auld Enemy at Hampden Park, Scotland stand proudly fourth and within striking distance, well four points, of Slovakia in second. Am sure they are still celebrating the Brownian u-turn al the way from Aberdeen to Wick and back again.

But more often than not these retirements are no such thing but more a rather pitiful and pathetic plea for attention, as if they do not get enough already. Sure as eggs are eggs or egos are egos, within a few months there is a call for the player to reconsider as there is a crucial match against San Marino for which they are desperately needed. They are implored to reverse their decision of just a few months ago to help their country in its hour of need as if they are the only ones who can possibly rescue the situation. Then we have the heart-rending, highly emotional statement that they are indeed returning to the fold and the bells ring out across the nation whilst the populace are busy hugging themselves in delight at this extraordinary volte-face. The player is naturally praised to the heavens for this, the ultimate in self-sacrifices and usually made captain to honour their remarkable transformation.

One can imagine the cohort of PR executives chuckling away as the collective rush of warmth towards the former-retiree approaches boiling point and congratulating themselves for getting their client back in the population's affections. Surely the BBC Sports Personality of the Year is on the cards and that unpleasant business with the chambermaid in that hotel is now thankfully forgotten and everybody is rightfully focusing on the wonders of his sensational international u-turn. It all goes to prove how you don't know how much you will miss somebody until they go.

Antonio Cassano's career was almost the definition of colourful with a variety of high profile moves to the likes of Roma and Real

Madrid keeping the erratic Italian never too far from the headlines. The end was suitably dramatic. Early in July 2017 Cassano joined Serie A side Hellas Verona for what appeared to be his swansong. The swan had hardly flapped his wings before he declared he was going to retire a mere eight days after signing. But good old Antonio was not finished there as just hours later he was back and he wanted to "have a crazy season."

After getting a couple of pre-season tucked into his belt and within a week of his renewed commitment to his new club, the 35 year-old had screeched into yet another U-turn and was riding off into the setting sun. Despite his wife Carolina's assertions that he would be seeking a new club after his stop start stop affair with Verona, Cassano gave us the definitive statement: "Carolina got it wrong. After thinking and reflecting in the end I decided – Antonio Cassano will not be playing football any more."

Another notable example of this rather poorly disguised exercise in attention seeking was performed by venerable midfielder Paul Scholes. Having enjoyed the fruits of a sell-out crowd at his testimonial in August 2011 following his announcement that he was retiring after 17 years at Old Trafford he made a comeback for Manchester United in January 2012. With some poetic justice Scholes' first appearance after his brief retirement was a 30-minute cameo that went some way to securing a 3-2 FA Cup win at Manchester City. Eventually Scholes and United missed out on the Premier League after that Aguero goal. Before this resurrection, Scholes' last game was the comprehensive defeat to Barcelona in the Champions League Final at Wembley so he clearly felt there was some unfinished business: "I've been pretty clear since I stopped playing that I miss it." And on he went for another 18 months, collecting his eleventh Premier League title, before calling it a day again.

Then there is the retirement home that is China that has become the natural habitat for those who find themselves considering their options and worrying about whether their pension pot is going to be sufficient to continue their rather comfortable lifestyle. Some will point to the import of Oscar a 25 year-old Brazilian international from Chelsea, who it could be argued is approaching his prime, as a sign that the Chinese Super League is not just a safe haven for old lags. But Oscar could be considered as the outlier in this equation and most of the players who wend their way East to Shanghai or Guangzhou and are well past their best and are feathering their nests rather than having any interest in developing their game.

Some of the figures quoted are eye-watering so Carlos Tevez who is not exactly a spring chicken at the age of 32 will receive £615,000 a week, or as somebody calculated, £1 a second. Even the Chinese realised this was the point when a reality check was urgently required. With the Chinese economy slowing down this sort of madcap spending, which the governing sports body described as "a grave phenomenon", is clearly not sustainable and the governing body have stepped in to introduce a spending cap. Chairman Mao Tse-Tung would have been so proud of such state intervention although he may have had a few qualms over the equality quotient involved in this redistribution of wealth.

At the top of that long, long run that gave batsmen plenty of time to contemplate their fate, there was a little shuffle and a look down for the mark and then the head would go back and the ground would float away as the silent strides settled the long, lithe body for the gather and release, everything pointing exactly where he wanted the ball to go.

*Gary Naylor in the Guardian on his recollections of
West Indian bowler Michael Holding in 1976.*

Michael Holding earned his nickname of Whispering Death because his run-up was so smooth that apparently it was not possible to hear him until his sudden arrival at the crease. The mixture of elegance and imminent threat became one of the iconic sporting images of the 1970s and was on a par with one of the most aesthetically pleasing aspects of football. There are few better sights in football than a direct free-kick arrowing into the corner of the net from distance. Paul Gascoigne's beauty against Arsenal in the 1991 FA Cup semi-final, Roberto Carlos' science-defying banana kick against France in 1997 Tournoi, David Beckham's last minute World Cup Qualifying salvation against Greece in 2001. Add to this illustrious list Cristiano Ronaldo who has shown the sort of sheer brilliance required to score such goals on dozens of occasions. Such goals stay imprinted in our collective memories and warrant endless replays to fully admire their intrinsic beauty. They even attract their own descriptive names such as the Tomahawk or the Knuckle Ball. They keep us warm during the cold winter months and can give us succour in the harshest of times.

But I do have an issue with Ronaldo's efforts, many of which are on the sumptuous end of the spectrum. The undoubted quality of the strikes is not the problem. The problem lies with what happens just prior to the kick being taken. There is a performance of such posturing, pouting preening that a peacock would blush, if it were possible. The attitude is that this is now all about one person and we should respectfully bow to his complete superiority. This is a gift to us all and mankind should be grateful. It goes a little like this.

As soon as the kick is awarded he struts over with the air of a man who will not brook any argument with his intentions. If anyone has the temerity to suggest they would be a better option, they are treated to one of those withering stares that is normally reserved for lesser beings. He sometimes even affords a sneering smile that is dripping with patronising condescension as in how could you possibly supplant me, you idiot.

If anyone remains within 10 yards of the kick, Ronaldo is likely to walk over and forcibly remind them of the need to get out of the way as he needs the space for his unlimited talent and does not need anyone cramping his style. The message is crystal clear, 'run along now you are not wanted here.' Once the stage has been cleared of these extras it is time to focus on the main act, the only act. This is the modern version of Shakespeare's seven ages of man.

Age One – The ball is placed with a precision that would normally be associated with a bomb disposal expert loosening the pin from a suspect device. Having taken the utmost care in setting the ball just so, spinning the ball in his hands to get it to the prime position for its future propulsion into the annals of the legend. This crucial preparation is followed by the stare.

Age Two – The intense stare is the first appearance of some psychological weaponry. The keeper is now targeted by those sharp gimlet-like eyes as he is singled out for special attention. Ronaldo lifts his head and focuses on the man who is about to be humbled by the mastery that is about to be unleashed. If the keeper is not made of stern stuff by now he will be feeling inadequate and questioning if he is the right position.He is basically already forlornly picking the ball out of the net.

Age Three – Having already reached a point of almost complete superiority, the nails are then driven into the coffin of the keeper with a nod of Ronaldo's head. This is not just any old nod but one that screams that you are no longer in control of your destiny and prepare to meet your free-kick taker. Nearly every keeper is now at a point of utter subjection to their lord and master, a whimpering wreck.

Age Four – With the keeper now in a state of such sheer panic that his head is spinning, his heart thumping and his knees knocking, it is almost time to take the first few steps backwards. Each step is taken so deliberately that it has a weight, a significance that goes beyond the mere physical action. These are further barbs into the soul of the already quivering keeper who is ready to be subjected to his fate.

Age Five – Suddenly the steps are halted and there is time for a moment of extended reflection in the middle of it all. He just stops and raises his head with even more deliberation and heft. Time is suspended briefly as the action freezes. After what seems like an eternity Ronaldo affords himself the luxury of another nod, this one slower than the previous one. It feels as though this one is born of a certain pity for the soon-to-be vanquished keeper.

Age Six – But that is enough of sympathy and it is almost time to deliver the fatal blow. The last few steps are taken with a degree of functionality as if it is now time to put the keeper out of his misery. It would be bordering on cruelty to extend this any further so speed is now of the essence. A couple of skips and we are on the point of merciful release.

Age Seven – The final act is upon us as the executioner reaches his appointed spot and having retreated to the required distance behind the ball, the hands are placed on the hips and with one final nod it is time. A couple of deep breaths allow everyone to gather themselves for the denouement. The world is ready and waiting.

Other than this, which is clearly a very individual aberration, there are another collection of run-ups that cause concern. These are restricted to the art of penalty-taking and those frightful penalty run-ups that Simone Zaza made instantly famous in the 2016 Euros with what can only be described as his epic failure. Having dummied his way to the ball he then lofted it way over the bar to the consternation of his team mates and to the delight of social media accounts across the world. There could be a new verb coined as a result "to Zaza", which is to make a complete and utter fool of oneself in front of millions of people. His season at West Ham featured none of the comic undertones and was just plain old boring shite.

A long time ago there was a rule that did not allow the penalty taker to break his stride, but that has been lost in the mists of time and so we have been exposed to the horrors of the stuttering run-up. This particular monstrosity was officially sanctioned by the International Football Association Board who confirmed, when outlining new set of rules in May 2016, that this was indeed allowed, as long as the taker does not actually come to a grinding halt as that comes under the bracket of 'illegal deception'.

There are quite a few players who now play that cat-and-mouse game whereby they slow down or tread as though they have hit a patch of treacle near the penalty spot in their approach to the kick in the vain hope that the keeper will for some unfathomable reason throw himself to the ground and leave a free passage into the net. This very rarely works and generally makes the taker look foolish and incompetent in equal measure. Good penalties are taken with a degree of confidence but these ones border on the criminal in their feebleness.

With such a fatal degree of hesitancy there is a shift in emphasis so the keeper is now much more in control than he might have been previously. With time to wave the arms around a bit, doing a couple of pull-ups off the crossbar, sing an operatic aria and generally engage in some off-putting antics the natural advantage shifts away from the spot kick taker who is rightly concerned about the lack of any momentum. The resultant kick is usually delivered with all the force of a light gust of wind and will end up in the clutches of the keeper who has to make every effort to resist the temptation of laughing and mocking the beleaguered opponent for his sheer ineptitude.

The generally quite good forward line at Barcelona otherwise known as MSN were culpable with Neymar in particular being fond of a stutter and their alarmingly low conversion rate for penalties can be attributed to their predilection for the stop-start run-up. Just imagine how many goals they would rack up if they took proper penalty kicks, so maybe this is a way of providing the necessary checks and balances to ensure that total domination is a bit further away. Maybe this is drilled into them that scoring penalties is just not the Barcelona way in that it is all a bit too pragmatic with very little room for the requisite flair and imagination expected of Blaugranas.

SELFIES

These Arsenal players need a reality check. Last season they celebrated finishing fourth at Newcastle and now they celebrate beating a Championship side on penalties – we are talking about Arsenal FC here.

Roy Keane on Arsenal players taking selfies
after FA Cup semi-final win in 2014

It is not often that Roy Keane is lauded as the voice of reason but on this occasion everyone can stand shoulder to shoulder with the irascible Irishman and hail his justifiable rage. One can only imagine what might have happened if someone had tried to take a selfie of the United team whilst Keane was still playing. Am not sure about the dimensions of a selfie stick but am pretty sure Roy would have made sure that it fitted nice and snugly into a highly personal but painful area of the anatomy of said miscreant.

As the world becomes more obsessed with self and the various egos scattered across the globe, the emergence of the selfie has become the perfect accompaniment to vanity. The very idea that having watched a match what we really need more than anything else is a series of pictures of the players taken by themselves for our delectation is one that defies belief. Is this really what civilisation has finally come to? Having spent the best part of two hours looking at their every move you would have thought we might have had enough but clearly we are poor, deluded souls. I suspect that somebody will justify this rampant narcissism by claiming that what this achieves is bringing the players so much closer to the fans and breaking down barriers. Poppycock and balderdash.

In a way the mass selfie in the changing room has replaced the autograph as the point of contact between the fans and their idols. But this method has the added advantage that there is no need for any physical interaction whatsoever with the great unwashed for the players or heaven forbid having to speak to them. Keeping them at a comfortable selfie stick distance is the perfect solution as it allows them to stay in their cosy, cocooned lifestyle whilst declaring that they are connecting with their fans.

If we fear for what is happening here, then spare a moment to consider what is going on across the Atlantic where in the MLS we have even witnessed the first yellow card for a selfie celebration. Hang your head in shame, Dom Dwyer of Sporting Kansas City, for this atrocity from July 2014, as this will be forever a stain on your character. What are the odds on the first 'selfie' to be taken in the showers with appropriately placed towels to hide their modesty? Or maybe the next stage in this evolution of nonsense is a player taking a photo of himself as he scores a goal, winking cheekily to camera. You heard it here first.

In January 2015 there were signs that some order had been restored when a few Premier League clubs, including Arsenal and Tottenham, announced a ban on selfie sticks inside their stadiums. For once Premier League clubs were making a stand for the man in the street but on a recent visit to the Emirates to see Palace's plucky 1-1 draw in April 2016, I did notice several offending items that had been sneaked in and so I fear there is still work to be done. I suppose if smoke bombs and flares can be smuggled in without too much trouble then the odd selfie stick will get through security, even at its tightest.

But there was something even worse happening in the country, which was much more widespread and consequently far more dangerous. Fans were being openly encouraged by other clubs to indulge in taking selfies. A prime example of this was Crawley Town who became the first team in England to introduce a sponsored selfie spot at their Broadfield Stadium (or as it is now catchily known, the Checkatrade.com Stadium, there's good old Checkatrade back again – see Dan Storey's C is for Checkatrade chapter) in 2015. Just consider those words for a moment – a sponsored selfie spot. Imagine making money from this ridiculous notion and who in their right mind would sponsor such a fatuous idea?

Quite rightly Crawley faced a barrage of criticism from across the nation for this flagrant lack of taste and within a month, announced that there was now to be a ban on selfies. The sting in the tale is that soon afterwards a club spokesman announced that they would renege on the deal and the ban consisted of quite warm air. "Anyone can take a selfie anywhere they like in the ground and even if they take on in front of the 'Don't take a selfie' sign, we'd turn a blind eye,'" Bruce Talbot backtracked furiously. He then made matters far worse by suggesting that Crawley might even run a competition for the most unusual location for a selfie. Confusion reigned and spare a thought for all those innocent people who just want to watch football without the horror of selfies being inflicted on them.

Going back to stadium security for a second I have a suggestion. I am not a fan of being too dictatorial about such matters but on this occasion I feel it is justified. As I remember the times when the only item you took into a ground was a scarf, a hat and maybe a rattle I urge the following action. From now on anyone attending a football match should have any hardware including their phone/ laptop removed before they enter the ground. After all Guardiola banned the use of the internet by his players at City's training ground then why can't we introduce something similar for fans.

The result of this is that they would not be tempted to spend the majority of the match tweeting, WhatsApping or whatever it is they are up to rather than watching the game. There was a terrifying picture taken at the Fulham-QPR match back in October 2016 when most of the fans were holding up their phones to capture a last minute penalty kick, which was consequently and quite rightly missed. That is what you call natural justice. And of course, most importantly if this ban was adopted there would be absolutely no chance of taking any selfies. Just an idea that could work out for the good of us all and even for humanity itself.

When I was young, I found out that the big toe always ends up making a hole in the sock. So I stopped wearing socks.

Albert Einstein

Here is that man Stuart Fuller again, who not only is chairman of Ryman South Lewes FC, has recently been appointed to the Supporters Direct board and is an author of several books including The Football Tourist. That is all public knowledge however what you might not know, as I only discovered while putting the finishing touches to this book, is that he has a vast collection of football socks. Yes that's right, a vast array of football socks of all shapes, sizes and colours so appropriately enough here he gets all tangled up in a messy combination of red tape and sock tape.

On the 3rd March 2012, the greater good of the beautiful game met for their annual meeting in the serene surroundings of Pennyhill Park in Surrey. Every year the International Football Association Board (IFAB), made up of representatives from the home nation associations and FIFA meet to discuss proposals for amendments to the rules. On this occasion, among the 8 proposed rule changes at item 5 on the agenda was one submitted by the English Football Association to Law 4 of the game relating to Player's Equipment.

I'm not saying that our regulators like change for change sake - after all I now sit in a position of rule making - but with bigger issues around goal-line technology and video replays it seems strange that the FA would feel that sock tape was such an important issue in the game that it required debate at this forum.

But debate they did and on the 31st May an edict was issued from FIFA HQ in Zurich to all football associations around the world which read:-

If tape or similar material is applied externally it must be the same colour as that part of the stocking it is applied to.

The reason behind the change in the rules was that an increasing number of players were using excessive amounts of tape externally on their socks. This at times had been a multitude of colours and completely changed the look of the sock. IFAB felt that this caused confusion, particularly for assistant referees who may need to look at the sock to determine who last played the ball before it went out of play.

There may be some logic in their reasoning but unfortunately as we know, football kit manufacturers do not produce kits in a standard range of colours. One look at one of their catalogues and you will see as many imaginative names of colour palettes as you will in the paint aisle at B&Q. If they had any sense, they would produce matching sock tape but they don't. Instead clubs have to try to match the basic range of colours that the tape is available in to their kits.

Last season in one particular Lewes fixture, kick off was held up after a major debate took place between the three officials over the "blueness" of our tape. Our away kit is a sky blue colour and the team had used, as they had done on numerous previous occasions, a royal blue tape. For the Assistant Referee tasked with checking the player equipment for the Rooks it seemed as if there were 50 shades of blue and he was using his authority to say our sock tape was in breach of the laws of the game. We were asked if we had brought our black socks (we hadn't) and whether we could wear those (we couldn't) and use black tape (we hadn't brought any).

Eventually, after the suggestion the players used clear sellotape was laughed at, the officials deemed that the tape was allowable and the game, a potential Play-off battle in front of an almost season best crowd, could take place. The fact that there was any potential issue due to some coloured sticky tape and the seriousness the officials took the matter was a niggle to say the least. Did the tape put any player in danger? No. Did the colour of the tape give us an unfair disadvantage? No. Would the tape colour have denied a clear goal-scoring opportunity or created a potential flashpoint in the crowd? No and No.

Back in the early Seventies the legendary Leeds United side started wearing sock tags, with their numbers and details of the game on in some instances. These blue tags were seen as revolutionary and were one of the smart touches that manager Don Revie loved to make his side look superior. Today, these would not be allowed as they would be in clear breach of the "rules of the game".

It find it amazing that this issue was deemed to be so important in the first place that it called for discussion at the table of the law makers, let alone one that requires our officials to have another responsibility.

Football is all about the 90 (!) minutes of play not the colour of a small bit of tape on their socks, especially when the colour of a player's boots is not brought into question. I'm a traditionalist and have only every worn black boots. Puma King's if you want to know the full details. But I'd like to know if the colour of socks tape (and undershorts) are such a concern to IFAB, then why aren't coloured boots, or is that simply because the boot manufacturers such as Nike and Adidas are major commercial partners of some of the world's biggest clubs and tournaments, whilst sock tape manufacturers such as Mueller aren't.

Iniesta doesn't dye his hair, he doesn't wear earrings and he hasn't got any tattoos. Maybe that makes him unattractive to the media but he is the best.

Pep Guardiola

I will come clean at the outset, I am not a fan of tattoos. For me they are mostly ugly blotches of ink that disfigure the human skin. Calling it body art is a blatant misuse of the word art and a blatant misuse of the body but I have been accused of being somewhat of a fuddy-duddy and a stick-in-the-mud, especially by my wife and two daughters who have all decided I was wrong and have ploughed on regardless with getting various tattoos on various parts of their anatomy over the last few years. My argument about how these will look when they turn the wrong side of 60 has gone unheard and I have to grudgingly accept that this is the way of the world.

For the sake of balance I interviewed Doctor Matt Lodder, Art Historian & Director of US studies at the University of Essex who is an expert on tattoos, having completed a PhD thesis on Body Art: Body Modification as Artistic Practice, no less. Dr. Lodder explained to me that it is not surprising that so many footballers have tattoos as the origins in Western culture are based on groups who wear uniforms, such as the military and prisoners. It is a way of expressing individuality when all their peers wear the same kit. This is a perfectly reasonable theory but my issue is that firstly we are not all prisoners or in the navy so surely the best way for players to express their individuality is to be quite good at what they do, such as Lionel Messi.

But even the revered Messi has slipped from his angelic perch in my eyes and gone for a variety of tattoos on his various limbs although almost inevitably, one of them is a rather sweet dedication to his first-born child, Thiago. Lionel, just buy him a silver christening mug and one of those napkin holders, it is far more preferable and classy to getting a tattoo and does less permanent damage to your skin and your reputation. Dr. Lodder leaps to the defence of Messi by pointing out that this is akin to having a photograph of your family on your desk at work. Then again you can easily pick up that photo of your loved ones and move it or even replace it with a better one. Alas with tattoos that option is not available and removal is either impossible or bloody painful.

As arguably the best player to grace this planet (See F for Fanboy) with his presence it is beholden on him to lead the way. If anybody does not need to express his or her individuality it is the gifted Argentinean. But then to make matters much worse Messi incongruously decided to cover his entire leg with ink, which sort of defeats the object of a tattoo as they are generally used to depict a particular image. So there goes his chances of the Ballon D'Or for another year or maybe he has finally seen the light and is now set on a course of steadily obliterating all previous tattoos.

Messi is also going against the grain of his beloved Barcelona, a club that has taken a stand against tattoos by banning any of the players who are accepted into their renowned academy La Masia from wearing them. So that begs the question what sort of example is their most celebrated player setting for those youth players. Then of course there was one other member of the MSN front line who is not shy when it comes to decorating his body, in fact he even went to the lengths of explaining every single one of them and their meaning. Just like Messi the majority of them are related to Neymar's family, no need for a family photo album anymore. He elucidated that the one on his left hand that simply says 'Love' is one of which he is particularly fond as his mother and father have it as well. Words sometimes fail me, which is not such a great attribute if you write for a living.

Then there are the religious ones, clearly Neymar is not content with his copy of Gideon's bible when he checks into his hotel room or crossing himself every time he crosses the white line or scores yet another goal. The Brazilian striker has to show his commitment to God by plastering every available piece of his flesh with messages including some choice phrases from the bible he revealed "I read every day." Maybe there should be an addition to the Ten Commandments – Thou Shalt Not Tattoo. Neymar also helpfully added that "all my tattoos are visible, I don't have any hidden." More's the pity.

There are numerous footballers who have also ignored my sage advice and have not been able to resist going down to their local parlour for some fancy needlework action. One of the first to go for it big time was that icon of football fashion, David Beckham. The media just could not get enough of what tattoo artist Louis Malloy was decorating his body with and judging from pictures of Beckham, he has not got many areas of his body that are left untouched. The last time anyone bothered looking he had a staggering 40 tattoos, all of which carry particular significance.

There are several religious-themed portrayals amongst the 40 of which the most worrying is the one on his left collar bone which portrays Beckham as a Jesus figure being lifted out of a tomb by his three sons, as cherubs. Eek, that's really pushing the deluded dad thing a bit too far. The overwhelming evidence suggests that footballers' tattoos are here to stay it seems so it is futile to resist but can we please have just a hint of decorum?

Perhaps the most outrageous and certainly one of the most idiotic examples came courtesy of the much-travelled Jay Bothroyd. Not content with having an alarming mixture of weapons, including a handgun and a grenade he brilliantly chose to get them arranged so they spelt out the word love. Talk about mixed messages, this was a master class and would have made more sense if he had selected a few doves and an olive branch to form the letters hate. One thing Bothroyd did prove was that travel does not broaden the mind. Just think, Jay when you have children having to explain those away to them. Even Dr. Lodder struggled to give any rational argument for this display of stupidity but he did point out that because footballers spend much of their youth in a bubble they will tend to make decisions that are not in tune with most of us in the outside world. Still, some bubbles are stranger than others, aren't they, Jay?

When supporters go down this route there are nearly always dire consequences. Whether it be a disastrous misspelling or even worse, dedicating a highly visible part of your anatomy to a player who suddenly ups sticks and joins a hated rival. In such a fickle and fluid world such as football it really does not pay to have your colours nailed too firmly to the mast, or the thigh in one fan's case. Robert Nesbitt, a Geordie suffered this indignity after having Newcastle goal scoring titan Andy Cole etched permanently into his thigh. When Cole left for Man United soon afterwards the resourceful Nesbitt did not hang about, adapting it to represent Les Ferdinand instead, leaving the rest of us suitably dumbstruck.

To add to the rogues gallery there is also the very sad case of the Liverpool fan who decided that it would be a right old jolly jape to not only have a tattoo of Adam Lallana but to go just one step too far and mix in a bit of a comedy pun whilst he was at it. And so we ended up with the spectre of the midfielder's face being merged into that of the domesticated pack animal, which swans around the Andes.

The emergence of Adam Lallama (sic) could well be the lowest point of this particularly gruesome pictorial history.

Then there is possibly the only manager in the Football League who has a tattoo and not just any tattoo but quite a collection adorning his arms. Step into the limelight Michael Appleton, former manager of Oxford United who joined the coaching staff at Leicester City in June 2017 or rather step away from the light, Michael. Whilst I have started to understand the predilection for players to get tattoos, courtesy of Doctor Lodder, I am a little baffled by a man in his forties having so many, perhaps this is just a symbol of a raging mid-life crisis but each to their own. I suppose in his pre-match talk, when he asks the team to put their necks on the line for the cause, he has something to back it up but am not sure Alex Ferguson would approve.

However, the very worst football tattoo is not on a player, a manager or even on a fan. When a referee becomes embroiled in this unholy mess there is very little material left from which to indulge in a good old bit of barrel scraping. The true horror of Mark Clattenburg's egotistical attitude to refereeing was on full display when he decided to have a depiction of both the Champions League and the European Championship to commemorate his double achievement in the summer of 2016. As a still bitter Palace fan I notice with interest he did not decide to mark the FA Cup Final in the same year with any tattoos. Clearly he could not see the advantage in such a thing, in the same way as he could not in the game itself.

Provocatively and predictably labelled as 'Clatt's tatts' this gives everyone with any agenda against the man from County Durham sufficient ammunition for a full frontal assault on his integrity and intelligence. As these two matches represent the pinnacle of his career, they are right in the open on his inner arms, so one wonders where the most appropriate part of Clatters' body would he care to have put the CheckatradeTrophy Final if he had ever stooped so low in his stellar career. I have a couple of suggestions, one of which I would imagine is extremely difficult to tattoo because of the lack of light and tight surroundings. But as his next career move encompasses that hotbed of football Saudi Arabia, the opportunities for even more radical tatts for Clatts are endless.

Truth moved beyond parody when US club Philadelphia Union announced that they were looking to recruit a 'chief tattoo officer'. The job spec reveals that the CTO (sic) "will be responsible for providing services to players and front office staff. Occasionally fan events will also be held with the CTO for the most loyal fans who want a tattoo to represent their passion for their favorite soccer club, the Union." So let's all form an orderly queue to get involved in those sensational fan events as they are bound to be pretty special by the sound of it, or alternatively shoot me now to save me from any more of this nonsense.

> TRIBUTES

The International Football Association Board (IFAB) states that players cannot wear "political, religious or personal slogans, statements or images." FIFA's secretary general, Fatma Samoura, in response to both England and Scotland wearing poppy armbands in November 2016 – "We have to apply uniformly and across the 211 member associations the laws of the game. Britain is not the only country that has been suffering from the result of war."

IFAB statement

There are undoubtedly many occasions when the football world rightly unites in respect and reverence for the loss of its brethren. The poignancy of an anniversary commemorating tragic loss of life such as the Munich Air Crash, Bradford Fire or the Hillsborough disasters are events that warrant a fitting tribute by the fans, players indeed everyone involved in the game. The tragic terrorist events in Manchester and London were rightly accorded minute silences at the matches that followed in their wake. All of them were impeccably observed and just proved that sometimes football does get things right.

A minute's silence, held before the match is the traditional way of paying respect to those who lost their lives and for the loved ones who have been left to grieve their painful loss. The vast majority of minute silences are similarly impeccably observed apart from the odd selfish attention seeker who cannot resist shouting out. Unfortunately there is nearly always one idiot amongst tens of thousands but they have been minor irritants in the overall scheme of things and tributes have been accorded due deference.

Recently we have had the trials and tribulations of Poppygate when the wearing of armbands displaying poppies for the England v Scotland game on 11th November 2016 created a furore. The FA stood firm after FIFA decreed that this was overtly political and as it prohibits political as well as religious or commercial messages on shirts, this was a clear contravention of the rules. Both teams were warned that they faced sanctions if their players wore these armbands. Cue moral outrage from some quarters and the whole storm dominated the build-up to a crucial qualifying match. Nearly everyone had something to say and the oldest international fixture in the football calendar was swept away in such an outpouring of invective about the suitability of taking a stand that Gareth Southgate and Gordon Strachan became bit part players in the whole drama.

Then the Welsh weighed in and decided not to risk the ire of FIFA by donning simple black armbands sans poppy and were subsequently accused of disrespecting the memory of all those who died and on the controversy rumbled on. Anyway good old FIFA were not fooled by this and launched an investigation into both the Welsh and Northern Irish over their more subtle poppy displays. It must be said that FIFA are nothing if not rigorous in their investigations of others misdemeanours, but slightly less so when it comes to anything to do with their own disorderly affairs.

The whole issue was effectively hijacked as Owen Gibson pointed out in the Guardian "If the whole point of Remembrance Day is one of quiet individual contemplation….then this unseemly episode seemed the opposite. Lurid tabloid outrage? Check. Cynical political point scoring? That too. A nagging feeling that the contrast between the manufactured controversy and the act of remembrance threatens to undermine the entire point? Yes."

Gibson neatly captures one of the key issues that has arisen out of the spate of tributes that the rationale behind the tribute gets mired in a war of words and tit-for-tat retaliations from both sides of the argument. When the prime minister weighed into the debate with her statement in parliament the die was well and truly cast. The row escalated into something unseemly and undignified which is the very opposite of what any commemoration should be about.

It is not just memorials for mass losses of life such as world wars. The tributes began for the odd individual to be commemorated for their services to football, such as after Sir Bobby Robson's death in 2009, which again was universally accepted but the method of commemoration had changed. It was felt that rather than silence, a minute's applause would be more appropriate. It was decided that this should become more of a celebration of an individual's achievements than the more sombre silence.It also made the odd idiot's attempt to derail proceedings so much more difficult as any shout would be drowned out by thousands of people clapping. Again this was all fine and dandy and nobody could argue with a great man such as Robson being afforded such a moment.

However, what happened next was that the number of people and occasions that justified such tributes suddenly grew dramatically and it reached a point when more matches than not involved a tribute of some sort. To accommodate this sudden explosion of tributes the minute's applause shifted from the pre-match slot to actually being held during the game at a pre-ordained minute. This was the point at which sentimentality was taking over from good sense and we were in a period of being too mawkish and allowing emotions to take over.

I have often wondered whether firstly this is a distraction to the players as the focus switches from the action on the pitch to the crowd and the person being remembered. Secondly, as I cannot recall a time when a goal has been scored during this minute, are players affected by this wave of emotion and do they deem it a little disrespectful to score during this period? Just imagine celebrating a goal at this crucial juncture, it would stick in the craw and be viewed as an interruption as much as the idiot calling out during a minute's silence.

In April 2013 a crisis was reached in the world of football tributes when it was suggested by a couple of chairmen, Dave Whelan of Wigan (who incidentally has a statue outside Wigan's DW Stadium) and John Madejski of Reading (who has a stadium named after him) that Margaret Thatcher's demise in 2013 should be honoured by holding a minute's silence. Now irrespective of one's political allegiances the very idea of a minute's silence for an ex-prime minister is one that steps over the line. Thatcher was such a divisive figure anyway but particularly over football, a game she saw as a social blight and in the late 1980s tried to introduce a national ID scheme that would have certainly reduced its popularity even further.

Most damning was the Hillsborough enquiry debacle, which took place on her watch and has only just been rightly exposed as the 96 received some element of justice nearly 30 years since that awful day in 1989.

To add fuel to a raging fire Richard Tracey, the sports minister at the time, had the gall to paint Thatcher as some sort of saviour of the game. "Football was in a bad way when she was prime minister, and we saw all the changes in her time, and they should pay tribute to that." Wisely, the Premier League and the Football League did not insist upon clubs falling into line and the thorny issue faded away. Maybe Whelan and Madejski could have picked some slightly less controversial figures, Pol Pot perhaps or even Atilla the Hun who would have been marginally more popular.

It is a delicate balance and one, which it is increasingly difficult to draw the line as to what or rather, who is worthy of commemoration. A conundrum that was neatly summed up by Chris Smith in his Football Pink column of March 2016 where he argued that a dilemma had been created about the appropriateness of such tributes after their exponential increase over the last few years and especially those commemorating non-football issues, including the Paris attacks of 2015 and the various terrorist incidents. Smith summarised it thus: "But I suppose the great hope would be for the traditional modes of reflection and the mood of the moment to find a more suitable, meaningful solution before the sentiment is lost entirely, and football becomes little more than a vehicle for falsified emotion."

As well as countless minutes of applause /appreciation we now have as regular as clockwork guards of honour for existing champions or long-serving players. Again the origins of this display of respect are slightly unclear but the idea has certainly become part of football's rich tapestry. The concept is fine in acknowledging the contribution of a fine team or an outstanding individual but when it comes to the execution things are not quite as straightforward. Take April 2013 as an example. Manchester United had just sealed their umpteenth Premier League title in the last umpteen years and were due to play at old but not really that close rivals, Arsenal.

Normally of course footballers are magnanimous in defeat and will laud their superiors to the skies but for once the Gunners were somehow a little miffed by the idea of giving United the full treatment. Their beef lay with their former captain who jumped ship from the Emirates to go to Old Trafford, and there was a lingering feeling of resentment that the Dutchman who had spent so many years in North London deciding to move to win the title that had eluded Arsenal for the last eight years Robin Van Persie had been there.

Some may say that the Arsenal players were being a bit churlish but why should they have to hide their natural disappointment of losing a long-serving player and former captain to a team that puts them very much in the shade? It is tough to show bonhomie when you are in such a foul mood and ultimately why should you be forced to do something just because it is felt like the right thing to do. Nobody could deny Leicester their moment of glory when they pulled off the most amazing title win for many a decade but did they really need two guards of honour, one at home to Everton and the other away at Chelsea? Surely this was over-egging the pudding. Of course there was the added frisson of Claudio Ranieri going back to the club that had jettisoned him a dozen years before and showed him very little respect, but all the same.

Then we had Steven Gerrard's departure from Liverpool, which was equally as well documented as Leicester's 2016 triumph and was accompanied with the now de rigeur guard of honour from the opposing side for his last game at Anfield in May 2015. Palace were not quite so accommodating on the pitch, maybe they had not read the script where they were meant to roll over and let Gerrard leave on a suitably euphoric note as he led the Reds to a rampant victory? Rather than being carried aloft on a golden throne to the adulation of the crowd after leading the Reds to yet another Anfield triumph, Palace proved to be party poopers as they ran out 3-1 winners ensuring that Gerrard felt a little miffed by the performance and the accompanying sense of anti-climax on the day. So much for the idea of a fitting tribute.

The last piece of this particularly unsatisfactory jigsaw is the one form of tribute that will never go away. We can ignore the minute silences/ applauses, we can avoid the guards of honour but we have to face this particular horror every time we go to the ground as it is permanent. I am talking about those ugly lumps of stone or brass or whatever material they choose to create these bloody statues. Statues used to be reserved for national heroes but the sudden adoption by football has become a worrying trend. One of the other issues I have with these monstrosities is that far too often they bear absolutely no resemblance to the person they are meant to be commemorating.

Take the Alan Shearer one that really gave absolutely no clue as to who it was meant to be apart from the archetypal one arm salute that the Geordie favourite made his very own. It is not as though this was an obscure, rarely seen celebration by some nonentity. The biggest flaw with this statue was the sculptor decided that he should turn it into a one-fingered salute, maybe that was in some way appropriate. The man scored 260 Premier League goals and the phrase 'Alan Shearer wheels away in delight in front of the

Gallowgate End' is firmly imprinted in every fan's mind, let alone somebody who is commissioned to sculpt this image for posterity.

The fundamental problem is that this and most other statues are crap and in the days of digital technology when 3D photocopiers that can turn images into actual solid objects, surely it should not be beyond the wit of man to get one of the most recognisable faces right. It could have been just about any other Newcastle player and there was much speculation at the time of the unveiling as to who else it could be. In the environs of St. James Park there are also statues to club legends Bobby Robson and Jackie Milburn so it is all a bit crowded and you cannot move for fear of bumping into one Newcastle icon or other.

But at least the Shearer statue problem was with the not so familiar face and the arm whereas Cristiano Ronaldo had one with a slight issue with something below the waist. The edifice that was erected in Portugal certainly stuck out in more ways than one and the figurine looked pleased to see everybody. One wonders why this part of his anatomy was the one that had been chosen as the one to accentuate. The only possible explanation was that the sculptor like many others thought that he was a bit of a cock.

Then there was the laughable Madeira airport fiasco as somehow the sculptor got it so badly wrong that there were fun and games to be had guessing who the brass bust most closely resembled because it was not CR7 that's for sure. When the suggestions range from Paul Gascoigne's buddy Ralph Moat through the whole gamut to Niall Quinn or Paul Konchesky you can appreciate how wide of the mark it was. The basic error in designing this was that there was a massive smile on the face, so this is clearly not anything connected with the Portuguese star. Helpfully at the same time they renamed the airport the Cristiano Ronaldo airport as to avoid confusion.

But, of course there is only one football statue that everybody remembers and it makes the toes curl just thinking about it. In the great wisdom of the owner at the time Fulham made the bold/ outrageous/ridiculous decision to have a statue of Michael Jackson outside Craven Cottage. Mohamed al-Fayed felt it was appropriate as Jackson was a good friend of his irrespective of how many times Jackson ever watched Fulham, but if it was more than one that would have been a major surprise.

But al-Fayed was not finished there and having sold out to new owners, who not unreasonably decided the statue bore little relevance to a West London football club and tore it down, the various misfortunes that befell Fulham including relegation from the Premier League were blamed on the removal of Jacko by their former owner. Over the years there have been some pretty ripe excuses for loss of form and status but this one takes the proverbial biscuit. You just know that somewhere out there is the odd delusional Fulham fan who imagines this might actually hold water and is preparing to bring the statue back to life to galvanise the team and get them back to Neverland, sorry, the Premier League.

Whilst I do not condone such behaviour when a Messi statue in Buenos Aries was cut in half there was a small part of me that sympathised with this action. Although Messi is not the type to make a song and dance about this there would be an entirely different response from one of football's other global stars. Naturally, the man with an ego that battles continuously with his talent, is going to have a statue dedicated to him after he carried off the Swedish Player of the Year for the tenth year running. That is not the most hotly contested prize in world football, I am not sure Sebastian Larsson's increasingly infrequent appearances make much of an impression on the judges for instance, but as they say you can only beat what is in front of you. So there will be a tribute erected outside the Stockholm Friends Arena and as the man himself rightly points out "It's huge for me. Most people do not get a statue until they have passed away." Precisely, Zlatan, precisely.

TROPHIES (FOR RUNNERS-UP)

THOUSANDS of Albion fans will get the chance to cheer their Premier League-bound heroes in an end-of-season victory parade. The club and Brighton and Hove City Council have confirmed that an open-top bus tour along the city seafront will take place on Sunday May 14.

From the Brighton Evening Argus

Here is the prolific Stuart Fuller (see N for Numbers and S for Sock Tape) who is directing his sharpened pen and even sharper wit at the idea that trophies are awarded to clubs who have not actually won anything.

Fuller is deeply concerned that rewarding failure can only lead to one thing and that one thing is not success. Our Stuart is not that keen on the Play-Offs winners getting the chance to drag themselves up those 107 steps to lift that shiny, be-ribboned cup that may be worth £200 million. As I have written The Agony & The Ecstasy (a comprehensives history of the play-offs) the comprehensive history of the Play-Offs I am duty bound to challenge Fuller to a sword fight at dawn at the Dripping Pan, home to his very own Lewes FC.

When asked once how it felt to finish runners-up in a race, legendary NASCAR driver Dale Earnhardt once famously said, "Second place is just the first place loser".

He's right. If you don't win, you've lost. Yet there seems to be a growing, niggly trend in football that everyone should be rewarded for something, almost like a children's school sports day where medals are awarded for participation and effort sometimes at the expense of performance.

I've no issue with the runners-up getting a medal or even a small memento for their performance but since when did the losers win a trophy? I first became aware of this on the last day of the 2016/17 Football League season when the EFL announced that if Brighton & Hove Albion couldn't better Newcastle United's result at Villa Park, they would be presented with the runners-up trophy after the game in front of their travelling support. Whilst I can't find an exact moment in time when this inclusive measure was brought into our game, it appears to have been in place for at least four seasons.

It's bad enough that a team finishing 7th in the Football League (League Two) can be awarded a trophy through the Play-Offs (isn't winning promotion in itself a just reward?) but to give out a trophy to a team who finished runners-up is pretty unique in sport, let alone football.

What next can we expect in our all-inclusive footballing world? A trophy for avoiding relegation? A trophy for winning a game that's not a cup final? A trophy for being the best behaved? Ok, so it seems we already have the last one through the Respect campaign.

I wasn't at Villa Park on that last day of the Championship season but I cannot imagine Brighton & Hove Albion celebrated with the same gusto of winning the league or a cup final nor will their fans have cared about winning a trophy - after all the prize of Premier League football next season is certainly a fantastic reward for their efforts on and off the pitch. In the week before the game few of my

Albion-supporting friends were aware there was even a trophy to play for.

Back in the 1990-91 season, or 2BPL (2 years prior to the Premier League starting) West Ham and Oldham Athletic went into the last game of the Second Division season, when the title of the league reflected the actual level you played at, both having a chance of winning the league. West Ham went into the game one point ahead of Oldham but defeat at The Boleyn Ground to Notts County opened the door for The Latics.

As the final whistle blew we invaded the pitch to celebrate promotion. Oldham were drawing at home to Sheffield Wednesday and the team would be presented with the Second Division trophy. Alas, Neil Redfern's injury time winner meant Oldham won the league. Did that dampen our celebrations? No. We didn't need a consolation trophy. It was slightly disappointing not to win the league after nine months of toil, but we were going up.

So my niggle with trophies for runners up is that we are trying to reward effort not achievement. Ultimately, football is about winning not being second best.

UNDISCLOSED FEES

According to the Premier League's official website, of the 115 permanent transfers (not including free transfers) involving Premier League clubs this summer, only five were disclosed with any official figure, meaning that football fans spent their summers reading an increasingly unwelcome, yet familiar phrase:... for an undisclosed fee.

Michael Butler, the Guardian 4 September 2013

We have all seen it buried somewhere in the detail of the announcement of the deal, the undisclosed fee. The very idea of an undisclosed fee immediately sets the alarm bells ringing as we question why exactly they are undisclosed? It is all a bit sinister as surely any fee should be transparent and above board if there is nothing to hide. It is not just the smaller clubs who are perpetuating this strange obfuscation, as Michael Butler of the Guardian explained above. So the stark and rather surprising fact is that in September 2013 only five of the 115 transfers involving Premier League clubs had officially declared the fee, which is a barely credible 4% and one wonders what the remaining 96% are up to.

Perhaps it is the amount of money that is making its way into the pockets of the agents that is a concern. That is indeed a legitimate concern as that can be viewed as a lot of money going out of the game and for the benefit of the very few. But as these payments have been going on for many years then that is not suddenly something that needs to be buried away, nearly everybody is aware that intermediaries are taking a healthy cut off any transfer otherwise why would they be involved? They are certainly not in it for the good of the game and this is not a mark of altruism on their behalf.

We have started to find out the eye-watering sums that some football agents are earning out of these transfers so the (im)perfect example was that Mino Raiola who trousered the not inconsiderable alleged sum of £41 million when Paul Pogba returned to Old Trafford. The fact that Frenchman's transfer fee was a world record £89 million was relatively small beer considering Raiola's cut was 46% apparently.

Then again it is sometimes in the club's interests to keep the final figure schtum as it could upset the fans to learn how much a player was bought for, or alternatively how little was received for selling one of the star players. It is often not in the interests of chairmen to reveal how they fared in the transfer market because they have made a complete and utter horlicks of the negotiations and because there are always two sides to every deal. So transparency is not on the agenda and will not be for the foreseeable future as long as there are those vested interests trying to protect their reputations from a good old-fashioned dressing-down.

Long gone are the days of true accountability and mutual respect for others in the modern world of transfers, surrounded by the mists of opaqueness to protect the image of those controlling the clubs as closely as they guard those transfer fees from the prying eyes of the pesky public. If football clubs were like ordinary businesses they would be expected to show the sale / purchase cost of assets (as players effectively are) but that is one big if and football clubs operate under their own rules so are not beholden to reveal what goes on.

There is also another factor in this increasingly murky business in that there are all sorts of adds-on, incentives, image rights and bonuses tied up with most deals and the mysterious other parties who are inextricably linked to the whole arrangement so that even the so-called 'disclosed fees' are not what they seem on the surface. One of the most high profile transfers of recent times was almost one of the more complex deals for reasons that became blindingly obvious. Neymar's transfer from Santos to Barcelona in 2013 was originally announced to be worth around €57 million, now naively you would imagine that Santos would receive the vast bulk of that fee but you would be sadly mistaken.

Only €17 million made its way to the selling club Santos, with the majority of the remainder going to N&N, a company set up by Neymar's father. Although that was apparently supplemented by a sort of pre-nuptial agreement that was sealed in 2012 where the Brazilian club received €10 million before any transfer wrangling. Even that €17 million Santos received was allegedly split three ways with third parties DIS and Teisa, who had part ownership of the Brazilian star. In the end Santos received a net figure of €9 million, which is less than 10% of the true amount after all those extras are included.

In 2016 Barcelona president Josep Maria Bartomeu admitted that the real figure was almost twice the original figure after various adjustments including a hefty "€5.5 million from the agreement with the public prosecutor's office and the State Attorney's Office." It is so annoying how ironing out those little legal niceties starts adding up. Bartomeu continued with the artifice. "Another thing is the overall cost of the operation. And this is an amount which is over €100 million." A classic case of how a statement leaves more questions than answers.

Any controversy surrounding a transfer of South American players has to be put in the context of one of the more bizarre 'undisclosed fees' ever negotiated. In August 2006 the Argentinean pair of Carlos Tevez and Javier Mascherano shunned the attractions of Chelsea to join West Ham on loan. The surprising nature of this double transfer possibly masked for a while the role of MSI and their president Kia Joorabshian in arranging the deal. But the attention of the world and especially the red half of Sheffield latterly was soon focusing on what went on behind closed doors as the Premier League launched an investigation the following March into the background to the third party arrangement.

West Ham were eventually landed with a sizeable £5.5 million fine but crucially avoided any serious punishment such as a points deduction, much to the chagrin of Sheffield United who were relegated at the end of that season chuntering on about injustice and generally getting the wrong end of the toffee apple. When all the shenanigans died down, nobody was any clearer as to what West Ham paid for Tevez and Mascherano and it remains a mystery to this day despite the close scrutiny to which the deal was subjected, proving that undisclosed very much means undisclosed.

Ultimately the truth behind transfer fees is very rarely seen by anyone apart from those on the inside. It is the implicit and explicit lack of trust that really rankles. The clubs do not trust anyone with the proper figures as that would be far too open and would even include the players themselves and others in the club as people who have to be kept at an arm's length. This is very much the mushroom theory of management, where you keep everyone in the dark whilst feeding them a load of shit. It seems to work for clubs like Barcelona so why not for others.

VESTED INTEREST

A strong personal interest in something because you could get an advantage from it.

Definition from the Cambridge English dictionary

Journalists do not evoke much sympathy from the general public and sports journalists in particular are considered to be extremely lucky as they have a job that entails what most of us have to pay to enjoy, namely watching sport. But there are drawbacks and pitfalls along the way. Here the Guardian/Observer London football correspondent Dominic Fifield, explains how uncomfortable it can be when you have to cover your own team and one's professional objectivity is put to the test.

So picture the scene. It is fast approaching 10pm on Monday, 5 May 2014 and, as Glenn Murray peels off Martin Skrtel to meet Scott Dann's hopeful punt with his chest, there is a collective in-take of breath to interrupt the raucous bedlam inside Selhurst Park. A gasp of glorious realisation. Dwight Gayle has been left in a pocket of space just outside the penalty area between a panicked Mamadou Sakho and Glenn Johnson, the latter's composure having long since drained. With all around him dazed and confused, the striker has a clear run on goal. There is an inevitability as to what happens next.

The frenzy of Crystal Palace's comeback against Liverpool that night, a blistering rally which culminated in Gayle's clinically dispatched finish beyond Simon Mignolet two minutes from time, arguably represents the highlight of the London club's most recent stay in the Premier League. They have dubbed it 'Crystanbul' south of the river, when a trio of late goals in nine minutes secured the hosts an improbable 3-3 draw and drained the last momentum from the visitors' pursuit of a first league title in 24 years. It was the kind of chaotic occasion which still sends shivers down the spines of Liverpudlians of a red persuasion but, years on, has Palace supporters punching the air. One of those "I was there" moments though, in this fan's case, one that prompted expletives rather than expressions of joy.

That requires an explanation. I was brought up a stone's throw from Selhurst Park and have therefore long been condemned to supporting Palace, but witnessed the pandemonium that night from the front row of the press box in the ramshackle main stand. My duties were to deliver an 800-word colour piece for the Guardian to accompany Daniel Taylor's match report, with the subject matter effectively predetermined: a Liverpool themed sidebar to be filed 10 minutes from time for first edition and, if necessary, "tickled" at the final whistle in case of any late drama. Watching Luis Suarez, Daniel Sturridge and Philippe Coutinho ripping Palace to shreds for 75 minutes would normally have been a traumatic experience but, with deadlines ticking ever closer, at least it made working life easier. I could blot out the humiliation, at least until I had filed, and concentrate instead on cold, detached professionalism. It was as if the script had been predetermined.

I was feeling relatively satisfied with the state of the copy as I pressed "send" with the visitors 3-1 up and Damien Delaney's deflected long-range goal apparently a consolation. Liverpool, still relentlessly on the attack as the piece was picked up in the office, were back at the top of the table. The pressure had shifted back on to Manchester City, and that first league title since Kenny Dalglish's team hoisted the trophy in 1990 remained a distinct possibility. An awkward hurdle had been vaulted, a first win achieved against these opponents in this corner of south London since 1997. It pretty much wrote itself.

The unsuspecting sub-editor was busy trimming and tweaking to fit the slot as Gayle set about taking a wrecking ball to Brendan

Rodgers' evening. While the home fans rejoiced at the equaliser, I recall pushing back on my wheeled seat, fingers dug deep into my scalp, with my own curse lost in the din. My team had revived to render my copy a car crash. Every instinct in me was to erupt in delight at what I was watching out on the turf though, in reality, the implications for the article were nightmarish. I simply had no idea how to react.

This job, as privileged as it is, can get in the way on occasion. Journalists have to try and remain impartial. Sure, we are constantly accused of bias, our Twitter timelines littered with accusations that we have deliberately slighted one team or brazenly favoured another. Often fans of rival clubs will point to perceived prejudice against their own within the same lines of an article. In truth, you actually take pride in putting emotions to one side to deliver balanced copy devoid of the heart-felt rant of the fanzine, or the knee-jerk reaction of the spectator in the stands. Yet, deep down, the attachment to a team never really goes away. That vested interest is always there. It is just controlled. Suppressed momentarily. Buried beneath the need to see the bigger picture. And, in all honesty, that can be infuriating.

It has denied me the chance to celebrate an FA Cup replay win at Anfield while another Palace-supporting press man, sitting at my side, inadvertently given me a dead leg with a punch of delight under the desktop as Julian Gray rasped in the visitors' second goal. It has prevented me celebrating Championship survival after a winner three minutes from time at Stockport County, and an excruciating post-match wait for the final whistle to shrill at distant Huddersfield Town. It has forced me to adopt the cold face at the Valley while surrounded on all sides by tickled Charlton supporters bellowing "We sent the Palace down" to the chorus of "Amarillo". Sometimes you want to scream. I remember a colleague that day announcing innocently "Well, that was fun, wasn't it?" as we squeezed into the press room for the post-match media conferences. No. No, it really wasn't.

Football is supposed to be a form of escapism, but where is the respite in the aftermath of your own team's relegation if the subsequent days and weeks are spent chronicling the demise? Supporters can try and forget for a while by seeking solace in a soccer-free summer, but the journalist has to pick over the dregs, all endless tales of players upping sticks, of the financial implications of the drop, and pained and constant reminders of what lies ahead. And, on the rare occasions things go well, what is the point if you cannot properly enjoy the most barnstorming of comebacks against title contenders?

There was no chance to revel in that remarkable three-goal salvo at Selhurst Park. Instead, once I had snapped out of my shock and coaxed out a phone signal, it was time to ad lib in desperation – "So now all Liverpool can do is hope etc etc" – while craving the chance to rewrite for the midnight edition. Clarity of thought might have come sooner had it not actually meant something. As much as being a supporter offers a level of empathy into the highs and lows through which fans go on a weekly basis, having an attachment to a team can also be a hindrance. This is no plea for sympathy given the sense of privilege I recognise comes hand in hand with this job. It's just that, on nights like that, a vested interest can be a pain in the backside.

VIDEO SCREENS

Following a lengthy and intricate process involving leading digital experts, the approved designs will add a new benchmark in world stadia, adding another marquee feature in an already iconic venue.

West Ham statement on its website, May 2016

Amongst the raging controversy and condemnation that followed West Ham's move to the London Stadium there was an unhealthy amount of hype about the multiple screens wrapped in and around the ground that gives "iconic venues" a bad name. This hoopla backfired on the Hammers when one of the key features of this display decided he was no longer interested on playing for the team, went on strike and upped sticks back to Marseille. The boastful announcement now looks a tad sad – "So expect goals from Dimitri Payet...". Oops.

With facilities ever improving within stadiums it is sometimes worth taking a step back to see if this modernisation is truly beneficial. One of those technological advancements that needs some re-evaluation is the unfettered growth of the video screen. Of course, it is fun to watch highlights on a decent-sized screen but there are plenty of drawbacks as well that need addressing pretty smartly or else we may end up in a bit of a tight spot. I distinctly remember the first such developments that went under ridiculous titles like the

Jumbotron and this was one occasion when size really did matter.

As an example, I experienced one of the more humiliating episodes in recent Palace history that was made ten times worse by the dreaded video screen. Back in January 2016 I slogged up the motorway to Villa Park on a wet and dismal Tuesday evening to watch Palace pick up the customary three points that were on offer from Remi Garde's hapless side. Beforehand in the local pub all the Villa fans were far too busy calculating how much they would lose by and when their inevitable relegation would be sealed, to have the slightest interest in whom they were playing.

And so, with a fair amount of confidence coursing through the veins we settled down for a nice, comfortable evening under the Villa Park lights. However, something rather odd happened after a goalless, sterile first 45 minutes, early in the second half when Villa mustered an effort on target. The Palace keeper, Wayne Hennessey was so shocked by this unlikely turn of events that after stopping Lescott's initial header he pushed the ball back between his legs and into the goal. If that was not calamitous enough the response from Villa's video editor was to replay the incident at least five times to prove that the ball had gone over the line even though it was at least a couple of yards over. The goal was never in doubt but clearly as this was going to be only their second league win of the season they needed to make the most of it and the replays kept coming long after the game had re-started.

That was really a particularly cruel way to punish the Palace fans and I am sure Hennessey must have cast the odd glance to one of those video repeats on what had befallen him. And here is the next aspect of the video screen to which I object. The players seem to be transfixed by watching themselves on the screen, even though they must have seen it thousands of times before, they still seem absorbed by it. Sometimes the restart is delayed as players gawp, open-mouthed at what has just happened. Just get on with the game and let's not dwell on the miserable performance of the defence, please. But there they all are, somehow transfixed by it all as if they have never seen footballers appear on a screen before.

But if the players are inexplicably bad then there are much worse to come from the fans who get some form of giddy excitement at seeing themselves and lose any sense of self-respect or decorum in an instant. Just watch as the cameras pan around and suddenly alight on somebody who then spots they are now on the screen. Having been previously inanimate apart from the odd pick of the nose they are magically transformed into gormless idiots. The resulting inane grins and over-enthusiastic waving is surely enough evidence to have them escorted out of the ground on the basis of diminished responsibility. This sort of behaviour should be discouraged but on they go with hardly a care in the world, making the most of their thirty seconds of fame.

And this is exactly what leads us to the next level of horror that we have to endure when the Fan Cam became a reality. Yet another transatlantic infestation, the American obsession with being seen on screen has made it over here that has led to a whole new generation becoming enslaved. Back in September 2015, during an England match with Switzerland there was a hoarding from one of the official sponsors Mars that simply announced "Seeing yourself on the big screen" as this should be some sort of life ambition and was a sure sign that we were travelling down a rocky path. Naturally, a few weeks later we had to witness the introduction of a Kiss Cam during the NFL game involving Kansas City Chiefs and Detroit Lions. This should have alerted us all to the dangers that lay ahead but nobody acted and we are all equally culpable. More fool us.

Wembley was inevitably one of the early adopters of a Fan Cam as the dash for cash continues to try and reduce the debt hanging over the national stadium. Having broken the mould, they insisted on making matters a whole lot worse by launching the first ever Dab Cam in the build-up to the game with Malta in October 2016. Just imagine being the very first person to be featured on a Dab Cam, how could your family possibly live that one down?

Whilst admittedly the FA did have their attention drawn to other matters after the Allardyce Telegraph expose and his messy departure, surely they should not have taken their eye off the ball so badly as to sanction this. Jesse Lingard was held partly to blame as he was one of the more persistent dabbers, and so after his inclusion in the England squad for Gareth Southgate's first international match, people started to add two and two together and they came up with a rather unpleasant result. What a way to mar(s) your full England debut at Wembley.

So the FA have admittedly made an absolute horlicks of this but then nobody was forcing people into actually getting involved in the Dab Cam. But there were unverified and unsubstantiated reports of people who voluntarily took part in this and there are even pictures showing adults indulging in these activities and quite openly smiling at the same time as allowing their own children to participate. I do not want to be too censorious or come across as taking the moral high ground here but one wonders if these people have passed the fit and proper test, and whether they really should be parents if they cannot control their children or themselves.

Now whilst the dab may not be the worst thing introduced by the French to these shores (Paul Pogba's massive price tag may have included a penalty clause for being such a prodigious dabber alongside his team mate Lingard). Although it is tricky to think of much worse, the Dab Cam is the lowest of the low. It is simply not acceptable to be encouraging people, including children, to act in this way. This sort of activity should be outlawed, not publicised. It is clear that the moral fibre of this once proud nation has been torn to shreds if this is allowed to continue and one shudders to think what might be coming next. Loo Cam perhaps where there is a live broadcast from one of the cubicles dotted around the stadium and the excitement builds as the door swings open to reveal somebody in the middle of a massive dabbing practice.

I wasn't kissing her, I was just whispering in her mouth.

Chico Marx on being discovered by his wife with a chorus girl.

I have always felt that there is something rather sinister about whispering. It is by definition not an open form of communication but there is more to it than that. The overriding feeling is of separation, it is a classic case of us and them, so if you are in you're fine but if you are out it feels bad being excluded from these inner secrets. Of course, the Bible tells us that the first whisperer was the serpent in the Garden of Eden and he was definitely not up to any good as he enticed Eve into the original mortal sin. Additionally, there is the surreal custom of horse whispering, which is accompanied by a strong sense of bedevilment. To sum it up, whispering is and always has had a touch of evil.

So when whispering became part of football it was clear that its malign influence had spread way too far. Forget diving or feigning injury the real rot set in as whispering became widespread both on and off the pitch. There are a couple of types of whispering that have crept surreptitiously into the game and have consequently besmirched football. The first is those wretched whispers that accompany any imminent transfer activity. When the infamous rumour mill starts to churn out players being linked with clubs, the Chinese whispers start to circulate where X is off to Y sparking a domino effect with A off to Z, B off to P, ad infinitum, which all remain so terribly hush-hush. The fundamental problem with such activity is that 99% of it is erroneous but that does not stop the whispers swirling through the ether and growing more fantastical with each repetition uttered so carefully under the breath.

The full impact of such behaviour is covered in more gory detail in the I is for ITK chapter so we do not need to dwell on it here. It is now time to focus on an even worse practice, one which has started to make a real impact on the game without any recognition or any form of resistance. Indeed because of the very nature of these dastardly acts nobody has seemed to notice the spread of such evil and therefore it is incumbent on me to bring it to the nation's attention before it becomes too pervasive and unstoppable. You will all thank me for this important public information eventually.

That of which I talk is the emergence of whispering between the players, but this is not just plain old whispering but something far more sinister. I am sure that whispering has been a part of the game for a while, passing on messages in secret is nothing new or particularly damaging. But we are not talking about just whispering, this is the conspiratorial version. This usually happens at free-kicks when you have the usual cast of two or three players who are jostling to take the kick unless Ronaldo is concerned when there is nobody to whisper to. There is generally an animated conversation between all the protagonists before some sort of consensus is reached.

Once there is agreement between the tight-knit group on the identity of the taker, this is when things really begin to kick off. The two rejected players who are clearly not exactly chuffed to the mint balls about being usurped decide that their advice needs to be treated as though it is a state secret. This is not only unnecessary but rather provocative. It is not as though anyone is going to be able to hear what the conspirators are actually saying but this does not stop the dramatic and over-deliberate actions of this cabal.

But they do not leave it there, witness the hand coming up to cover the mouth whilst imparting their pearls of wisdom. Not content with passing on information sotto voce, it is necessary to have a defence against any particularly sharp lip readers in the crowd who could suddenly crack the ever so confidential message. We are suddenly desperate to find out what it is they might be saying and although "Smash it in to the top corner", "Top bins", or "Just whack it" are not exactly revelations that will shake the world to its core they are delivered with all the covert, complex menace of a John Le Carre spy thriller.

This is merely the prelude to the next action where we really start delving into the dark arts. Not content with the previous efforts at disguise, the top of the shirt is now pulled up to cover the mouth as the message is passed on in an atmosphere suddenly full of subterfuge and intrigue. By creating an element of mystery where there is none, it makes us all rather suspicious and ultimately, this is exactly why the whispering started. The entire rationale behind the collective chicanery is to confuse and befuddle. In the act of being opaque the simple truth is hidden and our imaginations run wild with dastardly plots and schemes. Additionally there must be a particularly pungent aroma wafting through the nostrils as access to the sweaty body beneath has never been more intimate.

So when the ball is eventually curled towards goal the keeper is now going through all the endless permutations of dips and swerves that have been dreamed up by the conniving whisperers. Will it be an inswinger or a late dipper? So flummoxed is the keeper's mind that he is likely to allow a straightforward shot squirm through his grasp to the great delight of the trio of collaborators who run off to celebrate with a little huddle in the corner and the obligatory stage whisper. Just to rub salt into the wounds the poor keeper is now being assailed by team mates and crowd alike for his error, not through any whispering but by mass bellowing. And so the mind games notch up another victory in the struggle for supremacy and we end up with an extremely dangerous whisperer's charter.

———

WATERING THE PITCH

Play was then stopped when a rogue sprinkler at the Chelsea end started covering the pitch and some unfortunate Walsall fans in water, much to the amusement of the away supporters who sang is there a fire drill?

From the Daily Telegraph report on Walsall vs. Chelsea
23rd September 2015

We have reached an interesting point in football history when 'a rogue sprinkler' is responsible for halting play. It used to be the lot of the odd streaker or a floodlight failure to bring proceedings to a temporary suspension. But now we have the perfect example of how new developments in technology can get in the way as Walsall's high profile League Cup tie against Chelsea at the Banks's stadium. This may represent the moment when the machines started taking over from the humans and we need to be very wary of how this is going to play out.

As we all know, to our cost that the British love nothing more than endlessly debating the weather. It is a topic that breaks through our traditional sense of reserve and allows us to speak to literally anybody for a good few minutes regardless of how well we might know them. We know our place in the world order of weather, in a climate that experiences a disproportionate amount of cloud and consequently its fair share of precipitation which leads to the grass almost always being universally green it seems bizarre that there is an unhealthy obsession with watering pitches. It is not as though there is an imminent threat of the pitch turning into a desert instantaneously or that there is any remote reason behind such a decision.

In the old days watering was an underhand tactic to encourage a sticky surface that would slow the ball down and restrict the flow of a game when facing a superior side, John Beck was a master of the dark arts when he was in charge at the Abbey Stadium and was known to tinker with the conditions in order that his Cambridge United team's limitless procession of long balls into the corner were held up for his willing charges to chase down. This was merely one of many techniques that Beck employed in trying to put his own team into the best position possible by inconveniencing their opponents. Even the venerable Brian Clough stooped to underhand tactics by insisting on watering the pitch to upset the free-flowing Leeds of the 1970s.

Appositely it is where the rain remains mainly in the plain that some of the most recent examples of pitch tampering have been cited. There have been some feisty spats between Barcelona and both big Madrid clubs about how both Real and Atletico did not water the pitch sufficiently. But nowadays there is hardly a moment when the sprinklers are not in action, irrespective of the state of the pitch or the varying qualities of the opposing teams. Whether it is pre-match, half-time, or post-match there is never an opportunity missed to get them going.

There is nothing more incongruous and frankly irritating than arriving on a dank, dismal day with the rain coming down incessantly prior to the match to find that the blessed turf is being given a further dousing. It seems to be mocking us poor sods that are drenched as if to say you thought you were wet, well you've seen nothing yet. Of course the expensive drainage systems in place underneath many pitches mean that there is very little chance of flooding but it beggars belief why they need to do it in the first place. Actually there is possibly some rationale behind reaching saturation point.

The most intriguing part of the new systems is how they magically appear from beneath the surface and then just as you wonder how the various sprinkler heads have materialised they all of a sudden disappear from whence they first came not before they have immersed the pitch in a fine spray. My staunchly non-scientific mind has always marvelled at how this can be achieved and there is no longer a trace of this apparatus. Surely there should be a lump where they are hiding but on closer inspection they seem to have been gobbled up by the pitch, which is returned to its pristine flatness.

However, I digress this is clearly a nonsense and it is further exacerbated by the fact that the players are wearing what is as close to slippers as is possible in a sporting arena. So we are treated to the sight of so many million pounds of talent sliding on their bottoms continuously. Of course it would be logical if the slipshod stars were to change their flimsy footwear for something a bit more robust. But the sticking point is that they are no doubt barred from doing so because of some lucrative image rights / marketing deal that forbids anything quite so sensible.

Maybe they are auditioning for the latest sporting reality show – "The Slip" where they are judged on just how far they can slide. No doubt the stats guys are going to be rubbing their hands with glee at the prospect of another way to slice up a game as well as our friends in the graphic departments who cannot wait to get their technicoloured paws all over this (see G is for Graphics). I can also visualise the background music to this latest televisual extravaganza and the much-delayed return of Wet, Wet, Wet to the national consciousness. Oh my giddy aunt, make it stop now.

The biggest problem is that these new pitches with their hybrid blend of grass and artificial fibres produce such slick surfaces with barely a blemish and so adding water gives them a lustrous sheen that makes them look better in front of the television cameras. Not a thought is given to the fact that they have effectively created something that is akin to a skating rink to the poor unfortunate souls who are expected to perform on it. So bugger the impact it has on the quality of the game itself as long as it looks good on screen why would anybody complain?

Talking of television I have also discovered one other redeeming feature of this soaking affliction as there are those wonderful occasions when said sprinklers burst into life at just the right moment. It happens when the television commentary team decide to get close to the action and end up on the side of the pitch for their cosy fireside chat. Just as they start to pontificate about the game ahead their smug expressions are doused with an all-encompassing spray and however much they try to laugh it off you can just tell that underneath it all they are seething and that expensive haircut/ suit/ coat has been ruined. The beneficial side effect is that Robbie Savage will be throwing a major hissy fit. Marvellous. As pre-match entertainment it is almost as good as Martin Keown being smacked in the head with a misguided shot.

One must wonder where this worrying trend of excessive dousing will eventually end and I am pretty sure there is some clever so-and-so dreaming up a more spectacular way of watering the pitches of the future. This will probably involve a drone or two flying through the air accompanied by some ridiculous strobe lighting that will create a kaleidoscope of rainbows to entertain and amaze the watching public. Or perhaps there will be a helicopter hovering over the stadium and then showering all below with gallons of water. Welcome to the Chopper Dome. In fact the options are worryingly endless so remember where you heard it first, coming to a ground near you very soon. Naturally this will become the next in a long line of episodes that carry a familiar suffix and as all things are known as these days - #Watergate, a rather catchy title even if I say so myself.

X-RATED CHALLENGES

He pissed me off, shooting his mouth off. He was an absolute prick to play against. Niggling, sneaky. I did want to nail him and let him know what was happening.

From The Second Half, Roy Keane's autobiography.

We all know the type of tackle, they used to be described as crunching, as in crunching the bones of your opponent. It is the sort of uncompromising challenge that Roy Keane built a career on and ruined a few others including poor old Alf-Inge Haaland when he was on the receiving end of the Irishman's ire during a Manchester derby. As Keane described it so poetically in his autobiography "I'd waited long enough. I fucking hit him hard. The ball was there (I think). Take that you ****." That sort of brutal assault is what gives X-rated challenges a bad name.

Let's face it we all love a hard, uncompromising foul that clears out the opponent, there is that sense of bedevilment that every fan finds it difficult to resist. From the legacy of Norman 'Bites yer Legs' Hunter and Ron 'Chopper' Harris to Stuart 'Psycho' Pearce everyone loves a good, honest tackle; it is an integral part of the game and is as much of a skill as beating three players with a few step overs and a mazy run. The difference is that what separates X-Rated challenges from good, strong tackles is if there is malice aforethought as defined in legal circles. These are the nasty challenges that make you wince when you see the replay and it becomes almost too much for the soul to bear. Almost. But we get drawn towards it as moths to a flame. The fact that it is called an X-rated challenge makes the allure that little bit more enticing.

Remember the thrill of seeing anything X-rated when you were a kid, the lure of forbidden fruit that has always proved so irresistible to our basic human instincts. These are no namby-pamby 15 or PG style affairs but the proper hard core stuff that grabs you by the scruff of the neck or sometimes even lower. This attraction is exacerbated by the commentator who mutters under his breath that it looks so much worse in slow motion, usually in between the ninth and tenth repetition of the indiscretion as the broadcasters make absolutely sure that we have seen it from every vantage point possible. "Look away now if you are of a faint-hearted disposition" is of course a fairly unsubtle piece of reverse psychology that encourages 99% of the audience to draw their chair up that much closer to the screen and watch in even closer detail than is strictly healthy. There is that sense of a slightly dangerous, on the edge thrill to the idea, which can border on prying into somebody else's misfortune and that is a less than endearing trait of the average football fan.

The ultimate in this faux horror is then played out when a player actually does suffer an injury. The vultures circle as the camera zooms in to cover the wound in each and every gory detail. We really do not need to see the extent of the injury but in we go with forensic zeal to find out the true extent. "If I'm not mistaken that bone sticking out of the lad's sock is absolutely not in the right place and that angle is all wrong."

Remembering two of the worst, the appositely named David Busst at Old Trafford in 1996 and Djibril Cisse at Blackburn Rovers in 2004, still send shivers down the spine and every one of the other 205 bones in the body too. Admittedly neither of these were victims of bad challenges but actually bad fortune, and there were no close-ups of their horrible fractures at the time but one can only dare to think what would happen now. For a recent example, in March 2017 the assault on Seamus Coleman by Wales' Neil Taylor should probably have been classified as XXXX and we got to see it in slow mo and at every conceivable angle.

Naturally it would all be captured in glorious HD with the limbs in question being at the heart of the action. This would have the makings of an hour long special on the rights and wrongs of the offending tackle with accompanying analysis from a hastily assembled panel of experts. Obviously, it would be broadcast after the 9pm watershed to add that undeniable sense of X-rated frisson as nearly every conceivable angle is used to convey the true horror of what you will witness. This is why you pay your monthly subscription, after all, to get so close to the action that you are almost there so the pain is almost tangible.

There are even compilations of some of the worst incidents littering YouTube and various websites which attract their fair share of weird ghouls who somehow find pleasure in the grisly misfortune of others. They often turn out to be more popular than the Top 100 goals or a season's highlights, which is a sad indictment of the football world and proof positive that there are some pretty sick people out there. Now I am sure there are deep psychological reasons behind this sort of behaviour and it certainly does need some explaining, but that is not within the remit of this book, it is enough to simply observe and move on, much as we should do with this obsession with the more gruesome incidents.

A psychotherapy in which the patient recalls and re-enacts a particularly disturbing past experience usually occurring early in life and expresses normally repressed anger or frustration especially through spontaneous and unrestrained screams, hysteria or violence.

Definition of primal scream therapy from Merriam-Webster dictionary

It is one of those axioms that rings true in whatever field of life you are operating – 'The louder one shouts, the less one hears.' And this is certainly as true in football than anywhere else where the volume of certain people's comments is inversely proportional to the quality of its content. Generally the loud mouths in the crowd are the ones that so love the sound of their own voice, which is probably just as well, because nobody else does. By yelling at the top of their voice, they are certainly heard but rarely understood, as they tend to spew out the most unintelligible nonsense.

Having bemoaned the loss of atmosphere at grounds it may seem odd that yelling should be included in this list but it most certainly deserves its place. This is the sort of thing that can turn people off football entirely. The yellers are usually solitary figures; no doubt their companions have given up the ghost long before, ground into the dirt by the incessant drivel delivered by their former mate. It is not just the excessive decibels that alienate all within earshot but also the actual vocabulary that is liberally sprinkled with words that would make a sailor blush. It can also incorporate a special brand of moaning that is thankfully relatively rare.

The yelling begins long before kick-off as the players go through their pre-match routine to the ranting. 'You're not fit to lace my drinks!' is neither original nor particularly funny but it sets our man off as he emits a series of guffaws that makes everybody in the near vicinity start wishing for a temporary deafness as a preferable option. The yeller is not discouraged by the lack of response to his bon mots. And we are still over half an hour from kick-off. This is as painful an introduction to a game as you can possibly imagine and there is no respite. For just once in your lifetime you start yearning for some of that shoddy, incongruous pre-match entertainment involving a mascot and a set of massive rubber tyres, which might distract our tormenter-in-chief. But alas there is none to be had so we have the next instalment of the Yella-thon.

On to the pitch jog the unsuspecting match officials who are immediately assailed with 'You're not fit to referee' accompanied by a rendition of the charming ditty 'You fat bastard.' Apparently this is the height of comic invention but it seems to have escaped his attention that his 20-stone figure is not the sort that charms the birds out of the trees. Now the opposition hove into view, which sends our man into paroxysms of rage as he reaches boiling point as can be evidenced by his face turning a deep and rather worrying shade of crimson. Just as the St. John's Ambulance personnel start taking a keen interest in his welfare, he is off again and the voluntary medical staff turn away and head off in the opposite direction.

And on it goes as every character who enters the fray receives the benefit of the wit and wisdom of the yeller. There is not much to admire about this man but maybe a small nod of appreciation to his remarkable capacity to just keep going on and on and on in splendid isolation. If nothing one has to respect his stamina, if he had been another shape he might have made a pretty decent marathon runner. The justification for all this bilge is of course that it is just banter. Banter, now there is a word to make the toes curl. The notion of passing all this off just as harmless fun when actually it is the complete reverse being actually quite damaging and certainly not in the slightest sense amusing, is as misguided as any element of football support. Then when we move into the territory of 'bantz' or even worse 'mega bantz', it is high time to abandon ship.

Apart from a splitting headache and a severe bout of mind-numbing nausea the result of coming into contact with the yeller is the opportunity to relish the odd silence as he gathers breath for his next verbal onslaught. Never has been it so golden as in that moment of respite. Not that it lasts too long. "You're having a bloody giraffe." You check your watch and wearily realise there is another 80 minutes plus added time of this utter tripe to put up with. Of course there is the option of attempting to request that he gives it a break but that is like red rag to a bull as he has paid his money and he is as entitled as anyone else to his opinions. Who are you to tell him what to do, it's a free country etc. ad infinitum. Ultimately it just spurs him on so better to try and shut it out somehow.

There is one more problem with the yellers of this world in that somehow their voice always travels so effectively that is nearly always the only single one that can be heard on television above the general crowd noise. He usually picks his moment as to when to hurl his latest witticism into the mix and then it is broadcast to the millions watching on television, swiftly followed by the usual humble retraction from the commentator "I am sorry if some of you heard some bad language there and hope you were not offended etc." Well actually yes it was deeply offensive and welcome to our world everyone and you are going to just have to share our pain, I'm afraid.

Opinionated does not really cover it as that would seem to suggest that there is an opinion tucked away amongst the dross that is spewed forth continuously throughout the game. To describe this diatribe as opinions is really stretching it, as these are generally half-baked ideas with no rationale or even thought behind them just a continuous loop of ill-considered bile. One has to have every sympathy for the poor soul who has to put up with this at home as am sure he is not able to turn off the tap and we only have to bear it for around two hours a fortnight.

ZINEDINE ZIDANE'S EXIT

It was a difficult decision to send him off, but one cannot fail to recognise that the right decision was made.

Horacio Elizondo, the Argentinean referee who sent off Zidane in 2006 World Cup Final

If there was ever a man who deserved a grand exit it was Zinedine Zidane. Zidane was peerless, he was one of those rare footballers who transcended most normal divisions. Anybody with an ounce of football sensibility swooned at his magisterial presence on the pitch.

Whoever he played for whether it was Bordeaux or Juventus, Real Madrid or France, he was so good that he was a joy to watch even if he was playing for the opposition and you simply had to admire his talent. He even had a cool nickname, possibly the coolest ever; Zizou.

His goal in the Champions League Final of 2002 against Bayer Leverkusen remains one of the purest strikes of a football many of us have had the privilege of watching and one that you can never tire of seeing again and again. The fact that the ball came from such a dizzy height meant that for most mortals they would probably have tried to head it, and a select few might have had the audacity to try to trap it. But nobody would even have attempted to hit it first time because that would have ended really badly. But Zidane was having none of this and struck it with unerring accuracy into the roof of the net. The astonishing thing was that ball barely deviated so cleanly was it struck. The fact that all this was accomplished with his weaker left foot makes it all the more impressive. If ever there was a goal fit to grace an important game that was most certainly it.

Aside from his supreme goal-scoring ability, he also possessed a way of gliding over the turf that was almost balletic in its grace. He seemed untroubled by the other players around him as if they were merely bit part players in the grand scheme of things; as a result he used to run matches without ever looking as though he was breaking a sweat. It was if he was playing on a different planet to the others and he would be a must in most people's World XI. Indeed he was quite rightly voted as the best European footballer of the last 50 years in the UEFA Golden Jubilee Poll back in 2004. One of the few decisions made by UEFA that we can applaud as such a talent deserves all the adulation we can throw at him.

At a club level not only did he win the Champions League but he won Serie A twice and La Liga once whilst carrying off FIFA World Player of the year just the three times in 1998, 2000 and 2003. Having led France to both the World Cup in 1998 when he scored twice in the Final and the Euros in 2000 when he was voted player of the tournament there was little left for him to achieve. Even in his later years he had such a powerful combination of technique and elegance that he seemed to be always in control and serenely moving towards the end of his glittering career. What could possibly go wrong?

The 2006 World Cup Finals were set to be his swansong, as he had announced that this was to be his last international appearance. All went smoothly as France progressed to the Final swatting aside Spain, Brazil and Portugal along the way with Zidane scoring a couple of goals whilst carrying all before him. But the man, who was so talented and humble with it, will be forever remembered for his parting shot in 2006 World Cup Final when he pushed his head into the chest of Materazzi who went down like the proverbial sack of spuds. The referee did not spot it but the assistant drew his attention to the incident and Zidane was duly sent off. It was not even a proper head-butt as that would have been too brutal, too aggressive. Irrespective of the provocation of the wily Italian it was a moment of madness that stained his reputation. Even John Motson was outraged and labelled Zidane as a disgrace during the commentary.

Watching his dismissal is almost too painful for the soul to bear. He initially pleads with the referee but soon realises the error of his ways and is resigned to his fate. The sorry sight of him ripping off his sweat-bands and trudging off forlornly to never grace the football pitch again is enough to make a grown man weep. How did it all come down to this sorry saga? That this was to be the final act and the abiding memory of Zizou was a travesty. What should have happened was the glorious coronation of the true king of the sport but what we saw would have been a more fitting epitaph for the likes of Robbie Savage or Roy Keane. Never has a sending off been so inappropriate and it still rankles over a decade on, the sight of Zidane sloping off the pitch and walking past the trophy is one of the saddest images.

Of course this was not the only red card of his illustrious career, or even during the World Cup Finals, in 1998 he was sent off for raking a Saudi Arabian player. Overall he managed a total of a dozen dismissals and these even included the odd head-butt. He was no saint and there was a devil dressed in angel's clothing but who does not appreciate a wee bit of the darker arts and indeed it made sure that Zizou was not to good to be true as we had been thinking was the case.

To compound our collective misery is the stateliness of Zidane's own reflections on the incident. None of the self-justification or blind subjectivity that most would have employed and rather than castigating his tormentor or the referee he is rather harsh on himself. " It (the sending off) was a very good thing," Zidane told France Football. "It was good that Buffon signalled what I had done to the referee because it was not pretty. I don't know how I could have lived with it had France become world champions and I had stayed on the pitch." But that was what we all wanted more than anything else for you to be carried off the pitch and be paraded in triumph with a proper guard of honour [See T for Tributes]

The concept of self-effacing is not one that we normally associate with footballers and so this comes as a bit of a shock. But it is fitting that he should be the one that stands out from the crowd and distances himself from the majority because that is how he should be remembered, not the ignominy of his trudging off the pitch in Berlin's Olympiastadion. The last twist on this sorry tale was that despite all this Zidane was voted Player of the Tournament. Flawed geniuses don't come any better or sadder and this seems an appropriate point at which to mark the end of this book.